BLUE
CHRISTMAS

A Memoir of the
2010 Cholera Epidemic
in La Source, Haiti

ISBN 978-1-936208-37-1

Cover design: Lydia Zook
Layout: Kristi Yoder
Illustrations: Anna Etter

Printed in the USA
Second printing: February 2013

For more information about Christian Aid Ministries, see page 173.

Published by:
TGS International
P.O. Box 355
Berlin, Ohio 44610 USA
Phone: 330·893·4828
Fax: 330·893·2305
www.tgsinternational.com

TGS000617

BLUE
CHRISTMAS

A Memoir of the
2010 Cholera Epidemic
in La Source, Haiti

Katrina Hoover

Dedication

This book is dedicated to
Sandy Ridge Mennonite Church.

With special appreciation for:

- *your prayers while I was in Haiti*
- *Paul Miller, who forwarded the e-mail about Haiti to me*
- *Lloyd and Bev Mast, who arranged my travel plans*
- *the generous offering shortly before I left, when my purse was stolen while Christmas caroling*
- *the friends who took me to O'Hare at 2 a.m. and drove through a blizzard to pick me up again*
- *the check I found in my mailbox when I returned*

Table of Contents

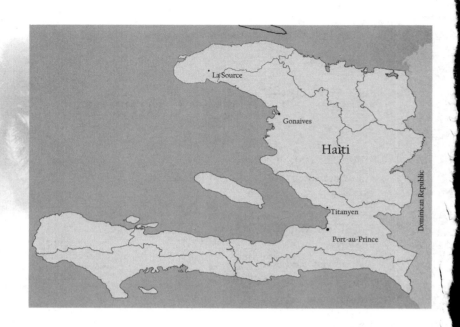

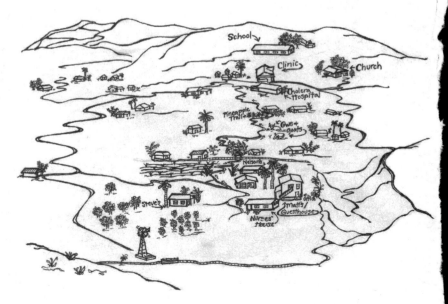

CHAPTER 1

BLUE CHRISTMAS EVE

Shining afar through shadows dim . . .

Everything in the temporary cholera hospital was blue. The walls were blue tarp; the beds were blue; shining through the tarp, the afternoon light was blue.

Two long rows of wooden beds, covered with blue tarp, stretched down the two sides of the hospital. The beds were arranged in sets of two pushed together, so that you could easily reach only one side of each patient. In addition, three beds had been placed in the center of the hospital, against cement pillars. The wooden beds had holes in their middles to save patients the trouble of getting up to use their buckets.

It did not stink. I was puzzled. Cholera involves large amounts of vomit and diarrhea. I wondered why the room with over a dozen cholera patients did not smell bad. Was it just a good day?

A little boy lay on his blue bed, mostly naked. Steve, the administrator of the mission outpost, handed the catheters to the staff nurses, Joanna and Bethanie. All three had lived in the La Source community for years and spoke effortless Creole, but they spoke to each other in English now as they gathered around the little boy, looking for veins.

I had been resting in my bottom bunk ten minutes earlier when Steve pounded on my door, asking for the 24-gauge IV catheters I had brought. They were a gift from a doctor in Wisconsin.

"They just brought in a little boy with sunken eyes, and they used their last 24 this morning," Steve had explained as I dug the small yellow box out of my luggage.

Long ago, someone numbered IV catheters and needles backwards: the common ones used in the cholera hospital were sizes 24 (small), 22 (medium), and 20 (large). With a young, dehydrated patient, the nurses did not want to try anything bigger than a 24. The small needles cannot provide fluid as fast, but there is more chance of getting them into tiny, constricted veins.

The situation sounded critical to me, and I did not expect to be noticed.

"You must be Katrina," Bethanie said, looking up at me from the patient's side. She was a tiny, hundred-pound woman, barely in her thirties. She crouched over the sick boy in a posture of urgency, yet I immediately sensed calmness.

"Have you put in IVs before?"

"No, I haven't," I admitted. Although I was in nursing school, I had no experience as a licensed nurse. I felt inadequate.

"You'll get to do some here," she said confidently, with a warm smile at the end of the last word, before turning back to the task at hand.

"Joanna," she said to the other nurse, "I'd feel better if you would do this one." I had read in e-mail updates that Joanna had an expert touch with IV starts.

Because the beds were in twos, Joanna could not reach the

boy's left arm from the floor. My nursing school brain, fresh from the sterile hospitals of South Bend, Indiana, was astonished to see her slip off her sandals and step lightly up onto the bed to access the boy's left side. Her youthful actions and refined features belied the few strands of gray in her hair.

The communication turned to Creole as the nurses tried to prepare the eight-year-old boy for the needle.

"*Pa souke*" (Don't move), they coached.

An IV needle is actually a needle with a tiny plastic tube around it, called the catheter. If the needle enters a vein, blood backs up into the catheter. At this point the nurse tries to slide the catheter off the needle and further into the vein. The needle is pulled out, and tubing is connected to the hub of the catheter. If the catheter is actually in the vein, the fluid will drip easily. If it is not in the vein, the fluid drips slowly. Eventually, and sometimes quickly, the fluid will collect in the tissue, causing swelling. This is called *infiltrating* and means a new IV needs to be started.

I gaped as the needle went in. The little boy did not cry; he barely flinched. Joanna probed for a few moments and got a flash of blood in the catheter. Bethanie handed her the IV tubing, and they started the flow to make sure it was in the vein properly. Pre-torn strips of tape were handed over by a tall, blonde girl whom I decided must be one of my fellow volunteers.

"We're glad you're here," she said to me.

With the IV running smoothly, we retreated to the nurses' station at the end of the hospital: a card table with a couple of folding chairs, across from a supply shelf made of wooden planks. Here too, everything had gained a blue tint.

"I like to give the new people a little ten-minute orientation," Bethanie said.

I thought of orientations back in the conference rooms of South Bend hospitals. At hours-long meetings powered by bottles of caffeinated soda and cafeteria muffins, we paged through stacks of stapled sheets and learned how to avoid lawsuits. By the end, the security codes and computer charting ran together, and the chairs had lost their comfort no matter how often we changed position.

I could handle a ten-minute orientation.

"Did you get a chance to research cholera?"

"I meant to," I said, embarrassed. "But it never really happened."

"I know how that goes," she said, spontaneously punctuating her sentence with another smile.

She handed me a stapled outline, a summary of cholera and its treatment.

The bacteria causing cholera descends on the intestines, causing them to drain the body of its fluids. All of our care centered on replacing the fluids lost by the vomiting and diarrhea.

In a description of cholera, Thomas R. Hendrix, M.D., writes that a victim of cholera may lose as much fluid as his own body weight through the course of the disease. Without fluid replacement, a severely sick patient can die from loss of fluid only two hours after the onset of the disease. As the fluid is drained from the bloodstream, the vital organs scramble to claim the remaining drops of blood. The arms and legs grow cold and pulse-less as the blood is saved for more important places.[1] Hence, getting an IV into a critical cholera patient and maintaining the flow of fluids was our single most important activity in the cholera hospital.

---

[1] http://www.ncbi.nlm.nih.gov/pmc/articles/PMC1749961/p.1.

Whether propped on a donkey, driven by a cycle, or carried in a bed, all patients stopped at the observation tent before entering the hospital. The observation tent was an extension to the main cement pillar structure. It was framed with poles and covered with more blue tarp on its top and sides. Another piece of tarp hung over the entrance, creating a makeshift door through which the Haitian breezes blew.

The first thing a staff member did was check for a radial pulse, the pulse that runs through the wrist in line with the thumb. If patients did not have a radial pulse, or if they did not have a measurable blood pressure, they were immediately admitted and started on IV fluids. If they did have a good pulse and blood pressure, a staff member recorded those numbers on a slip of paper and watched and rechecked the measurements for several hours. During this time they were given oral rehydration solution to drink. If they started vomiting, they were usually admitted, because of course it would not work to drink. If they were stable and did not grow worse, they were sent home.

"Thankfully, it doesn't have too much odor," Bethanie said when we got to the part about diarrhea.

So it wasn't just a good day. Nice.

She showed me the cardboard boxes of IV fluids and the Rubbermaid IV box with tape, catheters, and a blue tourniquet.

Each patient had two buckets: one under the hole in their bed for diarrhea, and one close to the head of their bed for vomiting. Both buckets were marked in liters with a black Sharpie.

If the odor was better than I had feared, the sound effects were worse.

"*Oi! Oi! Oi!*" a woman in Bed 2 moaned. The beds were

marked with yellow Post-it notes taped to the blue tarp or concrete pillars above them. Again, the black Sharpie was the inkjet printer of choice, and with it someone had written the numbers 1 through 24. Because the Haitian names were too difficult for short-term staff to pronounce, names were rarely used. Rather, we referred to patients as Number 16 or Bed 10.

"That woman you hear in Bed 2 just set a record for us last night," Bethanie said. "She had twelve liters out overnight between vomiting and diarrhea." She went on to explain that the woman had been at the hospital as a caretaker for someone else. When that patient was discharged, she began to walk home. Passersby found her collapsed by the roadside and brought her back.

"It can work so fast," Bethanie explained. "One man was found dead in his garden before anyone knew he had it."

"But with IV fluids it's very reversible, right?" I asked.

"Yes," she said. "We've had no deaths yet since we saw our first patient two months ago. Some were close, though!"

Bethanie explained that patients are expected to bring their own bed linens, pillows, and food. Their families help them clean up and empty their buckets after the output measurements at 6 a.m., 10 a.m., 2 p.m., and 8 p.m. Discharge from the hospital was based on output. Once patients had nothing in their buckets, they could go home.

"Clorox kills cholera," Bethanie said. "The families wash the buckets with Clorox water. And we use lots of hand sanitizer." Smile.

Orientation finished.

I couldn't help thinking how hard it must be to continually train in new volunteers like myself, only to see them leave again in a few weeks, and have to train another new person. "Isn't it miserable to have to train in new people all the time?" I asked Joanna.

"We're just glad for the help," she said graciously. "We could never do it without all the volunteers. God has been so good!" I had felt it the moment I stepped into the blue hospital: the welcoming atmosphere of smiles. Both of the staff nurses had a habit of smiling at the end of their sentences. I could tell they didn't realize they were doing it. I wondered if they developed the habit independently, or if they had influenced each other. I wondered how they managed to maintain it on their current 24/7 schedules at the cholera hospital. Whatever the case, I knew it was one reason why the blue hospital did not feel depressing, even to the new arrival.

I found out that Steve was originally from Ohio. He and his wife Deborah and their two boys had welcomed a new baby just three weeks before when Deborah gave birth to a little girl in a Haitian hospital.

Steve did not help with the actual IV start, but he seemed familiar with the proceedings and was quick to assist. This confused me, and I asked him about his medical background.

"I'm an observer," he said, laughing. "I find it interesting."

Although he had an air of business about him, I sensed that his daily routine had

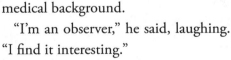
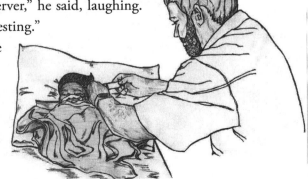

more to do with dust and activity than computer screens and office chairs . . . or "observing," for that matter.

Whatever their job descriptions, the two nurses and the administrator were working on a holiday. It was December 24, 2010. Except for my mental calendar, however, there was no sign of Christmas Eve. In the hospital, there were no manger scenes, no snowflakes, and no presents. There was no Christmas candy at the nurses' station, and no Walmart ads in the trash. There were no silver bells, gold ribbon, or red and green candles.

Everything was blue.

CHAPTER 2

CHICAGO TO PORT-AU-PRINCE TO LA SOURCE

Giving a light for those who long have gone . . .

The "Merry Christmas" throw was the only unnecessary item I packed in my suitcases. It made good padding for the more important things: the 24-gauge IV catheters, the gloves, the cheese to give as a gift to my hosts. To mark my suitcases, I tied them both with the red tulle I had saved from a Christmas gift. With two suitcases, I did not mind the luggage men at Port-au-Prince.

People will warn you about these characters, the ones in the yellow and navy plaid, short-sleeved dress shirts with slacks the color of split pea soup. "Don't let the luggage guys help you. They just want money."

But I was happy to give them money. First off, I had two suitcases and a stuffed backpack. Second, I had no idea where I was going. I ended up paying my helper $2, but I would have just as happily handed over $20. I would have never found my ride without him.

As we drove through Port-au-Prince, my guide pointed out the tent cities to me. Slightly less than a year after the January 2010 earthquake, the hillsides were still covered with blue tarps and tents wearing a year's coating of fine brown dust.

You could not help wondering how much thicker the dust would be when the "temporary" shelters were taken down.

There was not much sign of Christmas here, once you got past the red Santa caps worn by some of the airport employees. I had left the snow in Chicago as well; instead, there were silvery drifts of thin plastic food bags, with red or blue striping, blown into banks by the wind.

The next day I continued the journey north to La Source, traveling with Nelson and Rosemary, a young couple who lived in La Source. Nelson managed agricultural projects, while Rosemary gained the love of all the hospital volunteers by cooking evening meals and doing their laundry. Rosemary's sister and brother came with us, as well as Nelson and Rosemary's daughter Lovelie, an opinionated young lady of three years. Lovelie's adoption papers had not quite been finalized, but she was unquestionably theirs.

We passed Obama Beach, where Nelson wanted to point out a truck wreck. We never found the truck wreck, but I asked about Obama Beach. Yes, it had been named in the last few years.

Gonaives, the last town on the good road, was also a busy place. A large truck had lodged itself in the center of the main road, so for about ten minutes we inched through a massive bottleneck, with cycles threading through the tiny spaces Nelson left between the next vehicles.

After Gonaives, the earth became white and dusty and rocky, and the path was pockmarked with holes and ruts. With each jolt of the Land Cruiser, we headed farther into the barren wilderness. The landscape was better described by what was not there than by what was. There were no mile markers, no gas stations, no green lawns, no big tractors, no herds of beef cattle, no factories, no historical markers, no fast food billboards. The land looked like any part of the world would look, I suppose, if you would turn it on its side and dump everything off but small houses, chickens and goats, and people.

As the trail (I cannot call it a road) wound up into the mountains, the village children came racing out to the path and stretched out their hands, turned up, empty.

"What are they doing?" I asked.

"Begging," Rosemary said.

Little children, the same size as Lovelie, spent their days begging. They stood with empty hands between a barren earth and a vast sky, waiting for the white people or the rich people to come through with their vehicles. The emptiness growing inside me increased as I watched their attempts to find fulfillment.

We stopped at a roadside market and got lime sodas and fried *bannann* (plantain), still hot. I was glad that they actually had soda. It was even somewhat cold.

As we drove through the emptiness, I tempted Lovelie with the fresh cheese curds I had brought with me from Wisconsin. She did not really like *me,* per se, but she could not resist doing whatever it took to have more cheese curds. At last I had a moment of triumph, and she perched on my lap, even letting me snap a few photos.

We finally turned off the trail onto an even smaller one. Now we had to cross a riverbed four times. It was the same river each time—it had found the most comfortable position in the valley by doubling back on itself.

We were almost to La Source, and officially in the wilderness. Even Port-au-Prince, the poorest capital in the western hemisphere, was seven hours back.

Amid the brown of dust, the white of rocks, and the dusty green of cactus, there was just one other natural color, the shrubs with the orange flowers. No one seemed to know the name of the flowers. The shrubs looked like Dr. Seuss drawings, just twiggy brown forms with their arms stretched out, and round, orange bits of fluff for hands.

They were beautiful in a desolate sort of way. They reminded me of something I had learned in art class. Warm colors like orange and red rarely appear in nature. When they do appear, they are only there for a short time, like sunsets or fall leaves, or in small amounts like these Haitian flowers. Like the little children with outstretched arms, they were beautiful themselves; but standing against a backdrop of nothingness, they were too alone.

Dropped in the middle of this land of nothing, ringed by scarred and barren mountains, was the cholera hospital of La Source.

Anna, the tall, blonde girl, showed me around when we left the hospital. Since she was scheduled for the night shift, she soon retired to get some sleep. I had met Bethanie and Joanna and Steve. I briefly met Ethan, the third volunteer, who had come in when Anna did. With a week's experience, their seniority daunted me. Anna, Ethan, and I would divide each day's twenty-four hours among ourselves, just as Bethanie and Joanna divided each day between them.

Anna would report off to me on Christmas morning, and I would take the 7–11 a.m. shift. I would work again Christmas night from 9 p.m. to 7 a.m.

I did not remember ever having a physical pain of desolation in the pit of my stomach before, not even high in the mountains of Costa Rica, or on a rooftop in Puerto Rico, or on the moors of northern England. In those places, just as in La Source, we had been surrounded by strangers. We had lived in an unfamiliar culture. We had survived without McDonald's.

We. It had always been *we. We* had arrived on the same plane. *We* had experienced the culture together. *We* had complained about the bugs.

"I wish it weren't Christmas Eve," I confided to my spiral notebook. "I wish my friends were here, like in Costa Rica." I had gone to Costa Rica five months before, in August 2010. My mom, at the age of fifty-two, had died on July 24, 2010. In Costa Rica, I had felt the grace of God pouring over me through the kindness of my friends and the prayers of many people at home.

I had hoped that volunteering at the cholera hospital over Christmas break would be the same, a time to get away from the frustrations and shadows of life. As a nursing student, the experience would be valuable. But now, on Christmas Eve, as I lay on the bottom bunk in our closet-like room, staring at the wood and ugly floral fabric of the box spring mattress above me, the idea had lost its brilliance.

I spread out the "Merry Christmas" blanket I had brought and tried to get some rest.

CHAPTER 3

SERVICE TO SOCIETY

Fearless and tranquil, we look up to thee . . .

The generators at La Source provided electric lights and power to run refrigerators and computers, but they could support nothing that involved heat. There were no hot water heaters, no electric coffee makers, no microwaves, no toasters. And definitely no hot showers.

I went up to the nurses' house in the morning before my shift so I could follow Joanna down to the hospital. It was daylight, but I did not know the way. The path to the hospital was a meshwork of trails that broke off the main road at the end of a fence line. It led down to another fence line, where it was necessary to swing open a non-latching gate in order to enter a brief but narrow tunnel of thick path-side brush. The path curved out of this brushy area and spilled down over a hillside pasture heavily populated at all hours with goats, sheep, donkeys, chickens, and cows with perturbing horns. The path branched out in several directions across this pasture, and getting to the hospital meant taking a sharp turn to the right, at just the right place. At the end of the pasture, the trail took a little turn between two hedges of what looked to me like pineapples, but probably were not. It then came out by a house, descended past a tree where a friendly donkey was usually tied (when he was off-duty), and then came out into another open area.

The path descended more steeply from here, past one more house on the left, over a little bank and around a tree, before ending up at the opening flap of the hospital's observation tent. Preparing for the day, Joanna moved briskly around her kitchen. It was as if she knew eating was necessary—like buying gas for your car—but an equally annoying waste of time. She used a small filter in a mug and made her own coffee by pouring boiling water over the grounds. She yanked open the lower shelf of their gas oven and slid a piece of bread in to toast under the broiler.

Joanna came from a family of nine children. They had been raised in Ohio, but few of them had actually stayed there. They left to pursue missions in places such as La Source, Fair Play Wilderness Camp, Hillcrest Home, and New Horizons Ministries.

"What were your parents like?" I asked Joanna after hearing this astonishing census.

She laughed and shrugged. "They didn't live on the foreign field themselves, but they were always concerned about supporting the church and the ministry team," she said. "And they always supported us in our mission work."

Joanna had lived in La Source for eleven years. Following her down to the hospital that morning, I learned how to say

"Good morning" in Haiti. I knew that the proper word was "*Bonjou*," but I had much to learn about the way to say it.

It is impossible to explain on paper how the people of La Source say "*Bonjou*." Again, coming from northern Indiana, I can best describe it in terms of what it is not. Take out the clipped, quick tone of the "Good morning" you hear in the American business world that says, *I've got a lot to do today, and you are lucky that I have time to say "Good morning" to you.* Take the coffee and cinnamon roll out of "Good morning." Take away the rattle of keys and the click of computers and the beep of alarm clocks and smart phones.

The "Good morning" you have left when those things are gone is close to Joanna's "*Bonjou*" on the path to the cholera hospital. She and the people replying to her gave the word attention. There on the white, rocky path, with the morning sun spilling over the edge of the mountains, "good morning" was musical, relaxing, and non-threatening. Listening to her speaking to the boys on the path with their donkey or to the woman with a bucket of water on her head, you would never have guessed that she was actually an incredibly busy woman, about to take charge of the cholera hospital for the day. When Joanna and I got the report from Bethanie and Anna in the morning, we found out that a woman had died in the early morning hours. I remembered the patient from yesterday afternoon, struggling to breathe. Bethanie suspected that she was dying, not of cholera directly, but of a complication like kidney failure. Anna, who worked as an LPN on a respiratory floor back in Pennsylvania, had propped her up in bed to make it easier for her to breathe.

"I went over around 2:00, and she had gone into cardiac arrest," Anna said. "There was just nothing."

No one was surprised, but the first death was immensely disappointing.

Other than that, the night had been quiet.

"I could come back and help you today," Bethanie told Joanna. "I got a lot of sleep on night shift. Anna did a terrific job."

"You need some rest," Joanna said to Bethanie, with a smile.

"Oh, but I won't sleep if I do stay up at the house," she said. "I guess I could go catch up at the clinic. There's so much work piling up there."

"It *is* Christmas," Joanna reminded her.

"That's true," Bethanie said. She had forgotten.

Working Christmas morning in the cholera hospital was a crash course. Even if the morning would have been very slow, I would have felt a little unsure of myself, since it was my first shift and I didn't know what I was doing.

It was not slow. The observation tent filled with possible patients. Some of them were serious and needed to be admitted immediately. Even with her long night that included the death, Anna stayed much longer than she would have had to that morning. Ethan even came down to see if he could help, after hearing that we had four admissions at once.

After Joanna and I were alone, my anxiety went up a notch. Two or three IVs looked puffy, and I was not sure what to do about them. I wanted Joanna to look at them, but she was outside taking care of more new patients. One of the family members went out to talk to her about the IV. I knew that Joanna was busy and would come when she could, but I did not have the Creole vocabulary to tell the lady just to wait for her to come in. Also, I was not sure myself how critical the situation was.

When Joanna finally returned with a new patient to be admitted, the hospital was a chaotic mess of puffy arms, impatient family members, and IV bags that were nearly finished and would need to be changed soon. I had been wandering around, not sure what to do first, feeling the stares of the family members and patients watching me do nothing.

Why in the world is she here? I could feel them thinking. In fact, they were probably saying it too; I just couldn't understand them.

I decided to be honest with Joanna.

"I'm not sure what I should be doing," I said.

"Well," she said, glancing around the room at all the patients needing attention, "I think the priority is to get the IV in this little boy."

I tried to help Joanna as much as I could, even though I was not familiar with the procedure for putting in an IV.

Joanna took her time choosing a vein, especially with children. With light pressure, she moved her gloved fingers across a patient's arm, alert for that spongy, springy feeling of a nice vein. Sometimes, even during the day, it helped to hold our headlamp close to the skin to see better. Often she tore a piece of the glove off the tip of one finger to feel better.

When she found the vein, Joanna tore open a paper alcohol

swab packet and swabbed a large portion of the arm, up and down the vein if possible. She told me that it helps to start lower on a vein so that if it happens to blow, you can restart the line higher up the vein.

Then, with many soothing Creole words to her patient, Joanna slid the needle into the skin.

I stumbled along as best I could, with Joanna patiently coaching me about what she needed next. Hold the light, so she could see. Hand the IV line, so she could check if her access was successful.

"It's blowing!" she cried when the fluid started flowing. "Shut it off." That was something else that happened often, especially with thin or weak veins. The catheter was actually in the vein, but when the fluid started, the vein burst. She took out the catheter and searched for another vein.

When she did get in, she reached for tape, which I had failed to prepare.

"I'm sorry," I apologized, scrambling for the roll of tape. "I'm not familiar with the whole procedure yet."

"That's fine," she said with a smile.

Some people say "That's fine," and you can tell that it really *is not* fine, but Joanna said it like she meant it. She made me feel that, even though the tape should have been prepared at the beginning, she was so glad I was there to help, that she was willing to overlook the loss of the valuable time spent waiting for the clumsy nursing student to tear off the strips.

By the time we got the IV running successfully, Ethan had arrived to take my place and was helping me out by replacing several of the IV bags that had run out. I left my first shift feeling overwhelmed, but eager to learn.

. . . .

When it was time for night shift, I still wanted to follow someone to the hospital. I could maybe have found my way now in the daylight, but not at night. I closed the door to the guest quarters and walked up the short path to the nurses' house.

Bethanie was already preparing for work. As we chatted, I discovered that Bethanie had learned Creole as a child when her parents served as missionaries in southern Haiti. Eventually she decided to pursue medical missions. After studying at Columbia University in Manhattan, she reached her goal of becoming a nurse practitioner. She was now the head of the medical program at La Source and had lived here for five years.

Columbia University is a 250-year-old private institution with towering white pillars, manicured green lawns, and a reputation for excellence. President Theodore Roosevelt and President Barack Obama had both gone to school there. They, along with seventy-seven other former students, had won Nobel Peace Prizes. Bethanie chose to go there, however, not because of its prestige, but because she felt that it would prepare her well for medical missions.

As Bethanie prepared and ate her food with purposeful, efficient movements like Joanna had done that morning, the wind howled around the house. "Are we sure this isn't a hurricane?" I asked. The wind generators charging the batteries screamed in the wind. Occasionally, amid the gale, we could hear the long whine of a yard gate being opened, followed by a click as it was re-latched.

"This is normal winter weather for us." Smile.

While I had not expected to be cold in Haiti, I had a personal policy of never leaving home for long without taking with me my trusted, over-large, years-old Chicago sweatshirt. It was so old it felt like family, and I hated not to take it with me on trips. It came through once again in Haiti, where I huddled inside its warmth many times.

Close to the equator and surrounded by mountains, I found that night descended like a curtain being slowly lowered over the stage of La Source. In the brightness of the afternoon, you could see for miles. But when the light faded, you could see nothing at all. To me, the blackness was entire. However, on a clear night, the stars seemed to become unglued and drop much closer to us than they did back in Indiana. As we walked out of the nurses' house that night, I was glad I was following Bethanie.

"Do you have a flashlight?" she asked.

"No," I said. "Do you?"

"No, I know the path," she said.

"You really don't need a light at all?" I asked incredulously. There was an electric light or two up by the main cluster of buildings, but from there, the path snaked into the dark.

Bethanie laughed at my question.

"No, after every day for five years, I know this path quite well," she said. I was sure her sentence was punctuated with a smile into the darkness.

I was so busy trying to keep her white veil in sight that I did not want to talk.

"You'd better not stop fast," I warned. I brushed into things and tried to pick up my feet with each step to keep from tripping on invisible obstructions. I was downright scared. If I let her get more than a few feet ahead of me, I lost sight of her veil. I had no idea what to try to avoid at the edges of the path, or when we might come to the gate.

We would have been fine had it not been for the goat. His rope was caught on a shrub on one side of the footpath, and he was snoozing or having a late-night snack on the other side, his rope stretched tight across the path. Bethanie's foot caught the rope, and she did exactly what I had feared— stopped suddenly. Unable to prevent a collision, I fell on top of her, coming down hard on my right knee.

After we both said, "Are you all right?" and brushed ourselves off, she had a nice laugh. I was glad she found it humorous to have a clumsy stranger spill on top of her.

"I saw that goat earlier today," Bethanie scolded herself. As if she should have been expected to remember exactly where a goat rope stretched across the path!

We went through the little pineapple alley and came out by the house where the donkey was tied. From here we were close enough to the hospital to see the blue glow, created by the electric lights shining through the translucent blue tarp like an odd blue candle on a mantelpiece of dusty, white rock. The IV fluids dangling on their metal S-hooks, the scale, and other objects close to the tarp walls created fascinating and sometimes eerie silhouettes.

Bethanie and I were still laughing when we slipped inside the blue glow. I realized, as I bandaged my knee with one plain Band-Aid and one decorated with Dora the Explorer, that unexpected humor and spontaneous smiles were as much a part of the cholera hospital as the cement pillars, the pole observation tent, the pairs of beds, and the odor of Clorox. It was just one more reason why the patients passed other hospitals and clinics and kept on until they reached the blue glow on the hillside.

Since Bethanie also worked most of the day, she got as many hours of sleep as possible on the night shift. I tried not to stare as she curled up on a piece of cardboard on the cement floor, pulled a sheet and a fuzzy throw around herself and over her head, and went to sleep. Columbia University had kept track of their students who had gone on to receive Nobel Peace Prizes, the people who provided "service to society." I wondered if they had statistics on how many of their alumni slept on cement floors at night, surrounded by moths and the sound of vomiting.

This, I realized, was the world into which Jesus had come. A world where people with master's degrees sleep on the cement floor. A world of disease epidemics. A world of deaths in the night. A world where people hardly had time to eat.

Even geographically, La Source was like Jesus' world. A world of sheep on the hillside and complete darkness at night. A world with donkeys coming up the path and beggars beside the road. A world of desolation. A world where people forgot it was Christmas.

Borrowing Bethanie's e-mail account, I e-mailed my family and friends.

I am greatly comforted by . . . the thought that this Haitian world (dark nights, donkeys and goats darting, and sick people) is probably much more like the world that Jesus came to than the other world I'm familiar with (street lights, restaurants with nice napkins, orderly lanes of traffic, and brand-new hospitals). I have never been to a place before with beggars beside the road, as they were in the Bible. And I suppose Jesus' culture shock in coming to earth was much greater than mine in coming to Haiti.

CHAPTER 4

YOU'RE IN

Watching long in hope and fear . . .

There was a certain atmosphere that descended over a bed when we were trying to start an IV. All the tension and urgency of a cholera epidemic came down to just this one thing: an IV must be started.

Unless the IV was very non-emergency and easy, a second person usually helped. The backup person tore off strips of tape and handed new supplies such as catheters or alcohol swabs. When the needle person thought they were in the vein, the second person would hand over the IV line and then undo the roller clamp to see if the line would run properly.

Usually, if the needle person thought the catheter was in, it was. But it also happened that the cry of "It's blowing!" or "Stop it!" was shouted to the person manning the roller clamp. The tension would fall back over the huddled group of staff and family as the catheter was taken out and we searched for a new vein to try.

Only the necessary words were spoken. The more critical the patient was, the fewer trivial things were said. Everyone watching leaned forward silently, as if their concentration could somehow steady the fingers of the person with the needle.

Maybe the moral support of the observers did make a difference. One morning I was helping Joanna while she stuck a young man five times without success. She would get flashes of blood, but then they would disappear. The patient grimaced and turned his head with each stick, but there was nothing to do but keep on. Joanna looked up and down both arms and even took a look at his feet.

"I don't like using feet on men because they tend to have tough skin," she explained. Also, the danger of blood clots was greater in the feet.

Finally she told me to go get Bethanie. I hurried over to the clinic and hollered for Bethanie. She was in a back room.

"Joanna is having trouble getting an IV," was all I had to say, and she came immediately. Nothing was more important than gaining access to the body's central fluid system. The IV must go in.

When she arrived, the two of them crouched together beside the patient, consulting. They agreed that there was a vein on his left forearm that might still be an option.

"Do you want to try it?" Joanna asked.

"You go ahead," Bethanie said. Joanna was gloved up and in a good position. Both nurses were up on the bed itself, kneeling beside the young man's arm.

Joanna pricked him and got a flash of blood.

"There you go," Bethanie said.

"See, it does that, but then it quits," Joanna said. It was, after all, her sixth try.

"Try advancing the catheter," Bethanie said, so Joanna did, even though it seemed hopeless. She advanced and blood crept up the catheter. She withdrew the needle. A dark pool of blood collected at the hub.

"You're in!"

Those two words broke the tension. *You're in!* They were so musical, so rewarding, such a relief. Those words caused us to relax the muscles in our bent shoulders and straighten our spines. It meant that we could exhale, releasing the breaths we were holding. We could start picking up the trash: torn alcohol swab packets, empty needle caps, turned-inside gloves. In a case like this, there was likely a litter of retracted sharps to pick up too.

Maybe not as many sharps as attempts, however. Perhaps in the steel and glass hospitals of northern Indiana, it was protocol to throw away the sharp after every stick, but here we would occasionally re-stick with the same sharp. It was just one of the rules that was easier to remake high in the mountains of Haiti. We needed to conserve our stock of 22- and 24-gauge needles, and we needed to make time count. If every second of continued dehydration meant more recovery time and greater possibility for damage to the kidneys or other organs, the risk of infection was outweighed by the risk of lost time and resources.

. . . .

Severely dehydrated adults often received four liters of fluid wide open before we would adjust the drip rate at all. At wide open, a liter of fluid empties into the bloodstream in an hour or less, depending on the size of the catheter. If a 20-gauge catheter was used, the fluid flowed much faster than if a 24-gauge was used.

After four liters, it was common to back the patient down to 40 drops in 15 seconds (160 drops a minute). This was about the same as 500 ml/hr, so it would take about two hours for the bag to empty.

With no IV pumps, we were responsible to control the drip rate by setting the tubing's roller clamp correctly. Opening the clamp wider caused the fluid to drip faster, and tightening it slowed the stream. Sometimes we hit the correct drip rate with one twist of the roller clamp. More often, we would stand with our watches, glancing back and forth from the drip chamber to the second hand, waiting for it to come out right as we adjusted the roller clamp.

Since changing IV bags consumed a lot of our time, Anna had devised an efficient system. If we saw that Bed 18's fluids were getting low, we would pull a new bag from the box. With the trusty Sharpie, we would label it with the bed number and the drip rate: Bed 18 @ 30 drops/15 seconds; Bed 4, wide open; Bed 7 @ 10 drops/15 seconds. We would lay the new bag at the foot of the patient's bed for easy access. This helped us keep up with changing IV bags, which became especially important as our patient load increased.

Along with the race to stay ahead of the emptying bags, we checked vital signs (blood pressure and pulse) on all the patients every two hours.

. . . .

People came from hours away, they told me, to this hospital with tarp walls. For one thing, some of the Haitian medical facilities were afraid of cholera and not eager for new admissions. Furthermore, Joanna and Bethanie's clinic was known, respected, and inexpensive.

"They have some deep-set beliefs about fluids," Joanna told me. "For instance, they think you shouldn't drink if you haven't eaten."

Some of the Haitian healthcare workers shared these views as well. One of the local towns had lost 250 patients to cholera. Yes, it was a larger town, but not so large that 250 patients should have died. Joanna explained that part of the problem was the nurses themselves. Sometimes they failed to keep the IVs dripping at the proper rates. They would set them correctly when a knowledgeable director was watching, but that same person could come back later to find that the nurses had turned the rates back, believing the patient would be better off with a lower rate. If a patient who was supposed to be drinking lots of oral fluids fell asleep, they did not understand that it was essential to wake them to take a drink.

On the other hand, the patients' caretakers, usually family members, were quick to come to us at our card table nurses' station saying, "The IV fluid's finished," even when the bag still had enough fluid to keep on running for another fifteen or twenty minutes. They were uneasy if a line quit running, believing that it may be a sign that the person was dying or under a curse.

About a week before Christmas, seven-year-old Jidna came to the hospital. Although the girl's diarrhea grew less and less over her four-day stay at the hospital, she stayed lethargic. Her heart rate dropped. There were worms in her toileting bucket. Because of these details, Bethanie gave Jidna's father the choice of going home or staying one more night. Her father chose to stay.

That night, at 10:30, nearly a dozen people burst through

the tarp flap of the hospital and crowded around Jidna's bed.

Bethanie approached the crowd, speaking to them softly in Creole.

"Please, we allow only two people per patient at a time. We don't have enough space for more than that." She smiled.

"We're taking her."

"What?"

"We're taking her. She's not responding and the IV is not dripping into her. We're taking her."

Bethanie glanced at the drip chamber. It was dripping slowly, but that was because Jidna was almost over her diarrhea and the drip rate had been turned back to keep from overloading her little body.

She looked at the sleeping child, remembering the Haitian beliefs about fluids that stop dripping. How could she convince this determined crowd that Jidna had cholera, not a curse from an angry witch doctor?

"She's sleeping. That's why she's not responding, and we're the ones who slowed down her IV fluids. That's why they aren't going in faster. Look." Bethanie reached for the roller clamp, spinning it to the wide-open position. The fluids began to drip faster.

"We're taking her," the crowd insisted. They had been to the witch doctor, who told them that things were not good. The witch doctor had instructed them to come get the child, and they were determined that they would not leave without her.

Meanwhile, Jidna's father, who had been by her side all day and all night, was gradually waking up. He tried to orient himself to this sudden turn of events and unexpected group of visitors from his community.

Bethanie told the crowd the hospital policy.

"Well, I can't keep you from taking her, but I'm not disconnecting the IV from her because I haven't discharged her. If you want to take her, you can, but you'll have to take the IV out yourself. She's doing fine. I told her father she would be discharged quite soon."

When the father woke up enough to join the conversation intelligently, he remained firm in his decision to leave Jidna in the care of the hospital. He was eager to go back to sleep after watching at his daughter's bedside day and night for four days.

Finally, the delegation from the witch doctor slowly walked away.

Jidna got lots of prayers that night. Bethanie felt she was stable, but recognized that witch doctors sometimes do have power to predict what is going to happen. What would the people say if she died in the hospital overnight?

In a later e-mail, Bethanie shared the story. *I rested in the fact that Jidna, as I told the family, was under the care of Someone much bigger than even the greatest witch doctor. At our hospital she was resting under the wings of God. Jidna did make it through the night. She was discharged the next morning. I'm hoping the family chose to stay away from the witch doctor and trust in God, but I don't know what they decided.*

CHAPTER 5

THE ONLY WAY
TO SAVE LIVES

The Wonderful, the Counselor, the great and mighty Lord.

"There were so many times that we saw God working," Bethanie said. "So many times we were close to running out of IV fluids, and just at the last minute, we would get our new supply."

In normal practice, the clinic used about twelve liters of IV fluid in a year. When the first patient began to drain the tiny stock of fluids the clinic had on hand, a cycle brought another case from a clinic an hour away. That was soon finished too. Three more cases were brought by cycle from a pharmacy two and a half hours away.

As fluids continued to disappear, Bethanie next ordered ten cases from Port-au-Prince. This order seemed so large that Bethanie expected it to last for at least several weeks.

Before long, with treating adult patients who required a lot of fluids, the supply was getting low again. Word reached La Source that the pharmacy where they had gotten three cases was out of fluids.

Bethanie remembered a mission hospital that received medical supplies from Christian Aid Ministries (CAM), and a cycle was sent for two cases. Bethanie also e-mailed CAM's main headquarters at Titanyen, just a few miles north of Port-au-Prince. They promised to send a larger shipment of fluids, but this would take time.

When the shipment of seventy cases arrived from Port-au-Prince, the clinic was treating four patients and had only four small bags of IV fluid left.

So many things have worked out so perfectly, wrote Bethanie in an e-mail. *We haven't ever had an explosion of patients, forcing us to choose whom to treat and whom not to treat.*

. . . .

Besides providing the supplies for the cholera patients, God also provided the right people at the right time. At the beginning of the epidemic, when the nurses were finding their footing with the severely dehydrated patients, an ER nurse from the state of Georgia came to volunteer.

Tyler Yoder works at a Level One Trauma Center. While many nurses have never put IVs into the large jugular veins in the neck, Tyler inserts them all the time in the normal routine of his job. His skills with dehydrated patients were a major asset to the La Source nurses.

However, in Georgia, if an IV simply would not run, the ER staff contacted the surgery staff, and a central line was put into the patient. In La Source, Tyler realized, there are no backups. The life of each patient depended on inserting an IV.

Fourteen-year-old Wadlè came to the hospital early one Wednesday morning. The nurses evaluated him, and he drank oral rehydration solution. He continued to be stable, so they sent him home with instructions to keep drinking and to return if anything grew worse.

The next morning at about the same time, Wadlè returned. This time he had no radial pulse or blood pressure. His eyes were sunken and his hands were growing cold as the body hoarded its remaining fluid to the vital organs.

"We had a doctor and an ER nurse here at that time," Bethanie said. "The doctor couldn't get anything. Finally we called the ER nurse down, although he was not on duty right then."

At 6 a.m. Tyler awoke to pounding on his door and someone calling his name. He stumbled out of bed and opened the door.

"Bethanie wants you down at the hospital," Nelson said. "She radioed up to our house. They're not able to get a line into a patient."

As Tyler turned to go, Nelson added, "She wants a drill too! I'll get you one."

Tyler dressed at top speed, slipped on his sandals, and grabbed the drill.

What a beautiful Haitian morning, Tyler remembers thinking, looking out between the two mountain ranges to the ocean water beyond. He walked and jogged down the winding path to the hospital, past the donkeys, through the goat pasture, between the rows of pineapple-like plants.

"I also remember praying all the way down to the hospital, asking God, 'Help me get a line. If there is ever a time that I need your eyes to see a vein and your grace to steady my hand, it is certainly now,' " Tyler says.

He pulled back the blue tarp and stepped into the hospital, where the dehydrated young boy lay with Dr. Joel, a local Haitian doctor, bending over him. Dr. Joel had gotten an IV line in the left jugular vein, but it was not flowing well. On the bed, beside the litter of torn swab packets and used sharps, was a bent bone needle. The doctor had tried to screw the needle into the bone, but the pressure necessary to push the needle into the bone had caused the needle to bend.

While the doctor adjusted the tubing and put pressure on the fluids with a pressure bag, Tyler began to look for other options. With the tourniquet he methodically went over the boy's right arm, then his left arm, and then both legs. He saw the marks where Bethanie and Dr. Joel had tried to place IV lines, but he could not find any veins.

Even on very dehydrated people, there is usually something . . . a thin vein, perhaps only big enough for a 24-gauge needle. But on this boy, there was nothing.

"I guess we could do a cut-down," Dr. Joel said. "Bethanie, do you have a sterile scalpel?"

At Tyler's ER in Georgia, cut-downs are rarely used anymore, but even there they are done occasionally if fluid cannot be put into the veins or bone any other way. In a cut-down, the doctor cuts through the skin on the inside of the elbow so that the veins in the arm can actually be seen. The IV is then put directly into the vein.

Wadlè was getting more and more lethargic. Although he had tried to drink the oral solution, he had vomited it. There was only one thing to do, and that was to get a line into a vein or bone.

Bethanie ran to get a sterile kit for the doctor. The doctor went to look for a tiny drill bit, hoping to sterilize it with flame. This would be another option. They could drill a hole into the boy's tibia, the bone below the knee, and place the bent bone needle into this hole.

While they scurried on their errands, Tyler moved to the boy's neck, still searching for a vein. As he did so, the morning sun shone in through the open end of the hospital, as if God Himself was leaning over the dying boy and the caretakers who were trying to save his life.

When nurses put jugular lines in at the ER, they hit a button on the electronic bed, and it tips the patients' feet up and their head back. They hope this will cause the veins in the neck to fill with blood and stand out.

With no electronic switches and no Creole interpreters close by, Tyler raised the foot of the bed and nodded to two male family members standing by to hold it in place. He showed the boy's mom how she could hold him against the blue tarp bed to keep him from sliding down off the head of the bed.

With two fingers Tyler placed light pressure just above the collarbone on the right side of the neck. There was nothing. He moved to the other side, where Dr. Joel had placed the needle that was not running. Again he applied pressure just above the collarbone, and this time a gentle curve in the skin showed a vein, right beside the other needle.

For a moment Tyler looked up into the faces around him: the two men, holding the foot of the bed; the mother, keeping her son on the board; the crowd of other family members and friends who had joined the desperate procession to the hospital in the dark. All of them watched his every move with silent, intense eyes.

Under this pressure, Tyler breathed another prayer to God for guidance and grabbed the largest needle he could see in the box, an 18-gauge. He held it for a second, then dropped it back and took the slightly smaller 20-gauge instead. *No need to get too ambitious*, he remembers thinking.

He tore the paper and plastic sleeve away from the needle

and set it down close by. With the fingers of his left hand, he put pressure back on the vein.

Still there.

He picked up the needle with his right hand and uncapped it with his teeth. Breathing a prayer, he slid it under the skin.

He felt the subtle *pop* of the needle puncturing the vein wall. Then blood raced into the catheter, reached the end and began dripping. Tyler gently slid the catheter in as far as it could go. With a syringe of normal saline, he flushed the line. He could feel the fluid rushing past his fingers into the vein. With lots of extra tape, he anchored the line and started a liter of lactated Ringer's solution flowing into the boy.

Praise the Lord!

It had taken an hour and a half to gain IV access.

Twenty-four hours later, by the blessing of God and the skill of a volunteer ER nurse, Wadlè was discharged again—truly healthy this time.

CHAPTER 6

BEGINNING

Star of the East, undimmed by each cloud . . .

At the end of October 2010, the first cholera case came to the clinic. It was after hours when a messenger came and warned the nurses that a man with diarrhea would soon be brought in on a bed.

At that time there was no blue-walled cholera hospital. The nurses saw many patients each day at the white and green clinic. The clinic was a bustling place where a number of Haitians were also employed.

La Source had no clinic at all until Joanna came in 1996. As a practicing registered nurse, she was familiar with the medical field, but starting a clinic was a whole new world. She spent a year learning the language, becoming familiar with the culture, and going from place to place to find ideas on how to operate a clinic. Her brother Bobby and his wife also lived in La Source at that time.

At the beginning there was no permanent clinic building in La Source, and Joanna began seeing people on the long porch of her brother's house, where Bobby's wife did her laundry with a wringer washer.

On the first "clinic" day, Bobby, who was more fluent in Creole at the time, helped Joanna with communication. After that, Joanna was on her own, with a Creole dictionary in hand.

"Their porch and yard were full of people," Joanna remembers. "I think the people came more out of curiosity than anything else. Most of the people did not seem very sick, but it gave me a chance to learn the language."

In the process of developing the clinic, Joanna met with the leaders of La Source, asking them what they would like to see there, and telling them about her vision. She stayed a month with an American midwife living in Haiti. She toured other clinics in Haiti to gain insight and ideas. She flew to Tyler, Texas, for a Mercy Ships conference on mission medicine.

Meanwhile, a family in Ohio who lost a son in a farm accident offered CAM their son's savings to build a clinic in La Source. With the help of locals and work teams from the States, the Joshua Memorial Clinic was built and officially opened its doors in June of 1997.

In 2005, with the clinic well established and running smoothly, Joanna moved back to Ohio and Bethanie took her place as head nurse. However, two years later the clinic was again in need of a nurse and Joanna moved back. Bethanie remained the head of the medical program.

In many cases this would have caused a power struggle. Joanna, who had been in charge of the clinic for years, was now second in command. However, she graciously recognized Bethanie's more extensive training. She could often be heard saying, "I'd feel better if you would talk to Bethanie about that," or "Bethanie did such a good job with . . ."

No one noticed this more than Bethanie herself. "The fact that it works for her to be here working under me and not being in charge of the very thing she created says a lot about her," Bethanie says.

Together the two nurses kept the clinic running smoothly, seeing about two hundred patients per week. The clinic charged a flat fee of $10 Haitian (about $1.30 U.S.). This covered both the consultation and any necessary medications. While other area clinics had only a $2 consultation fee, they would then charge another $40 or more for necessary medication. Furthermore, many of the local clinics did not have a good stock of medicine. With donations from the States, the La Source clinic was able to consistently provide inexpensive medical care.

Each day of the week had its special focus.

Tuesday was prenatal day. Expectant moms paid for their first visit, but after that they did not have to pay for care and teaching. At the clinic, the moms were taught how to care for a newborn. They were tested for HIV and syphilis, diseases that can be passed on to the baby if precautions are not taken. All moms who received prenatal care at the clinic and who presented their baby's birth certificate after they were born were given a layette bundle, sent from sewing circles and individuals in North America.

Wednesdays were set aside for children. Besides routine vaccinations and countless severe rashes, a lot of children were malnourished. Sometimes a baby's mother had died and the family could not afford to purchase formula.

A malnourished child was given twelve cups of beans and rice ground together, a few cups of oil, and a liquid nutrient drink. They were asked to come to the clinic every two weeks for weight checks and their next food ration. Small babies were given formula. "We consider ourselves very blessed that most of the time we have infant formula like Similac on hand to offer the families of these infants to help them live," Bethanie said.

Occasionally, a malnourished child's family members would take the food and eat it themselves. One skinny boy haunted Nelson and Rosemary's house. He lived under the same roof as his stepmother and was treated poorly. His half brothers and half sisters did not like him, and they always took the food. Rosemary began feeding him a daily meal from her own table.

There was a day for HIV patients and tuberculosis patients. Besides this, every Monday and Thursday people of all ages and conditions came. Usually there were too many patients to see, so an employee decided who would be seen and who would have to wait. Forty-five patients a day was the most the clinic could handle. There was a wide variety of situations. The clinic had seen cases that ranged from mild to severe, from headaches and rashes to heart disease and machete wounds.

When the messenger came to the window on that evening in October, Bethanie and Joanna had already put in a long day. Furthermore, they did not expect to see a true cholera case.

"We knew the cholera was coming," Bethanie said. "But I kept checking with the neighboring town. I assumed cholera cases would show up there first, and then we would be next. As long as they didn't have any, we weren't too worried."

When they carried the man into the clinic, diarrhea was pouring from the bed like water. Definitely an indication of cholera. With fluid draining so rapidly from the body, the diarrhea and vomit from cholera patients look like potato water.

The man had vomited once in his garden that morning. He

went to the river to wash, but on the way back from the river, he had started with both vomiting and diarrhea. By the time they brought him to the clinic, he was too weak to sit upright on a cycle. Because he lived about three miles away, it had taken two or three hours to bring him to the clinic on a bed.

The man had no detectable blood pressure and no radial pulse. With her stethoscope, Joanna listened for the man's apical pulse, the beat heard over a person's heart.

"She couldn't hear it," Bethanie said, "and she's really thorough! Then I listened, and I couldn't hear it either."

"No apical pulse? And you brought him back?" I asked.

"We did," Bethanie said. "God did." She smiled. "Joanna got an IV into a little vein, and then once we got some fluid into him, we were able to get into a bigger vein."

I could imagine the scene. The tense silence, the rattle of IV catheters being torn from their paper and plastic pouches. I could imagine the hurried, hushed commentary. *What size do you want? . . . We'll never get anything bigger than a 24 in there . . . These veins are so constricted . . . What about his hand? . . . There are some really thin ones there, but we could try . . .* And then, the electrifying words, *You're in!*

How thankful they must have felt to hear an apical pulse come back!

And did the nurses realize that they stood at the top of a vast wave of cholera patients that would not peak until Christmas week?

The man stayed at the clinic until he recovered. For the first three days he had no urine output at all, a dangerous sign of damage done to his kidneys. To their relief, his kidneys recovered and began to produce urine, and he was soon released.

In early November, as the patient load increased from one or two at a time to four or five at a time, the clinic staff began to wonder what they would do if the number of patients continued to rise. Steve enclosed the back porch of the clinic with tarp, and mats were put on the floor for three patients. Two of the four exam rooms in the clinic also became patient rooms. With this arrangement, up to six patients could be handled at one time, with the clinic still seeing its normal load of other patients.

The first patients all came from four communities close by. However, Bethanie knew that as the epidemic progressed, new zones would be affected. *There are dozens and dozens of other communities for which we are the nearest healthcare facility with IV fluids. Many patients would probably die before reaching the next closest facility,* Bethanie e-mailed to the rest of the CAM staff.

Realizing that the patient load could soon mushroom beyond the space of the clinic, Bethanie suggested that they find a bigger building to use as a cholera hospital. If that was not possible, they would need a plan to transfer the patients to another hospital.

About a month before, a government-funded market building had been started across the road from the clinic. Although it had no roof yet and the floor was not finished, it looked like a perfect place to have a temporary hospital. It was only twenty yards from the clinic.

At a community meeting on a Friday, Steve presented an offer to the people of La Source. If the community would give permission to use the building for a temporary cholera hospital, CAM would put on a good tin roof and help finish pouring the floor.

The people agreed and the floor was poured on Saturday. Building materials and additional workers from CAM's main base made the long, violently bumpy trip to La Source on Sunday, and on Monday morning the work began. By Tuesday night, when the workers returned to the main base, the hospital was finished. The roof was on, blue tarp was securely fastened to the sides for walls, and the first cholera beds were in place.

Again, the hand of God could be seen in the perfect timing. The day before the hospital was finished, the clinic had seven cholera patients.

Bethanie wrote in an e-mail, *It is such a blessing to have Steve, the administrator here, coordinating all those aspects of the project—and such a blessing to have our Titanyen staff constantly shipping more IV fluids and other supplies up here for us. We feel so blessed to be so well equipped. So many other facilities really need this type of help too, and can't get it.*

CHAPTER 7

WHATEVER WE HAVE

Still bright o'er the cradle, and bright o'er the grave.

For the last few days the nurses had been dropping worried comments about the baby in Bed 14. The baby's cry was very weak. This was her third time back at the cholera hospital. Her mother, who had HIV, seemed to be caring well for the baby while at the hospital. Yet the scrawny arms and legs, and sparse, unhealthy wisps of hair suggested a lack of nutrients.

Bethanie and Joanna told us that, a week prior to her first admission, they had given the mom a month's supply of formula for the baby, who was about seven months old at the time. When they admitted the little girl a week later, the mother said the milk was gone.

"Obviously she sold it or otherwise misused it," Bethanie said.

"So what was she feeding her?" I asked.

"Well, we observed her giving the baby sugar water with cheese curls in it during her first admission," Bethanie answered.

The baby had been restless and unhappy all night. She did not have an IV in place, because the first one had been ruined and no more veins could be found. Bethanie and Anna finally put a nasogastric (NG) tube down her nose in the middle of the night to make sure she got fluids. Putting in the tube had been a hassle. NG tubes are supposed to slide in through a nostril, down the esophagus, and into the stomach. This tube was so tiny and slender that it kept curling, coming out the other nostril or out of the baby's mouth. Finally they tried a slightly larger, heavier tube. This one went to the stomach. They anchored it securely to the baby's face with white tape.

When I arrived that morning, the baby was scheduled to be fed every half hour. Because her stomach was too small for much volume, we gave her only 20 or 30 ml (about an ounce) at a time. To make sure that the tube had not slipped from the stomach, we checked for placement each time by blowing a little air into her stomach with our large feeding syringe. We listened with our stethoscope for the sound of the air in the stomach.

The baby's radial pulses had become difficult to feel, and her fussing had become weak and mechanical. Her belly was sticking out in an unnatural, distended shape. The mother continued to put food in the baby's mouth, such as spoonfuls of gruel or rice.

"She's only nine months old, and she's feeding her rice?" I asked Bethanie.

"Well, rice is good for stopping diarrhea," Bethanie said. Better than cheese curls, I supposed.

Bethanie thought it possible that the child had HIV or AIDS herself. Not all children of HIV-positive moms have the same condition themselves. If it does present itself in children, however, it can progress very fast.

Maybe it was my uncertainty with the tube placement that caused the mom to crack that morning. Maybe she suddenly became overwhelmed by the responsibility of knowing that she had fed the baby cheese curls instead of milk, realizing that she had not been the world's best mother.

It was time for the baby's feeding, and I was listening with my stethoscope for the whooshing sound as I put air back into the stomach. I just did not feel confident that I was hearing it, and I did not want to go ahead with the feeding until I was sure.

"Bethanie, can you come confirm me on placement?" I called to the nurses' area.

Bethanie came and we both bent over the baby, feeling the distended stomach, checking for placement.

Patients and their families are experts at reading the expressions on the faces of healthcare workers. I knew this from having been a patient once myself. It is not a good feeling to see multiple people suddenly scurrying to your bed, especially if they look confused or worried.

The mom began to wail the death cry. Tears formed in her eyes, and she bent over on the bed, hiding her head in her hands. Coming from the composed American Midwest, I had no experience with this, but I knew what it meant.

Bethanie spoke to her, scolding her gently in Creole. It is amazing how much we can tell from tone of voice. I never asked Bethanie what she said, yet I knew what she was saying. "You can't give up hope! The baby's not dead!"

The other ladies in the hospital jumped up too, making soft sounds with frowning faces, as if to say, "Stop making such a fuss; it will be okay." Bethanie informed me that grieving is not socially acceptable in Haiti. Perhaps there will be a big clamor when someone dies, but for the most part, people do not want to see other people cry.

"I helped at the birth of a stillborn baby," Bethanie said. "When the mother started crying, everyone else said, 'Don't cry, don't cry.' I told them, 'Let her cry!' Even though they may be sympathetic, they feel it is not healthy for a person to cry."

Quiet tension filled the hospital. In Bed 13 there was another little girl, probably three years old. Her mother was a classy woman who rarely left her daughter's side and insisted that the little girl say *"Mèsi"* (Thank you) when given a balloon or ribbon. This woman, with her elegant, lacy head scarf wrapped around her head, had been full of smiles the day before.

Today, with the mother in the next bed beginning the death wail, this woman also became tense, refusing to set her child down. The three-year-old was drowsy, and she tried to wake her.

"Just let her sleep," Bethanie coached the lady with the lacy wrap. "She didn't get much sleep last night."

From that point on the HIV mom gave her baby up for dead. She called her husband to come so they could take the baby home to die. She stayed outside the hospital most of the time, letting the other ladies look after the baby.

I wanted to hold the baby too. She arched her back and tossed her two small arms into the air. I knew that in storybooks babies reach their arms to heaven before dying. I wondered if she was going to die in my arms. She did not. Her lungs continued to fight, pumping out ragged, sob-like breaths.

There is something incredibly wearing about listening to someone's lungs fighting, when you are pretty sure they are going to lose in the end. The baby may have been scrawny, but her lungs continued to breathe, as if her body refused to admit defeat. The rhythmic grating noise was rapid too, like a machine determined to provide the needed oxygen to the cells.

The tube feedings were just not keeping enough fluids in her. We changed the schedule to every fifteen minutes instead of every thirty minutes, but still her radial pulse could hardly be felt. Her heart rate dropped into the 90s, beating with a tired sound.

It would have been better to have constant IV access than to feed her with the tube. Also, the mother had requested to have the tube taken out, because she did not like it. She thought it made the baby more uncomfortable and made it harder for her to breathe. It was definitely ugly; we could not argue with that. Bethanie had explained that we had been unable to find another vein after the first IV.

Bethanie took the baby to the nurses' station. As she sat by the card table in the blue morning light, she ran a finger lightly over the baby's forehead.

"I think this is a vein," she mused, stroking the brown scalp. "We could try."

Watching her fight to breathe was almost more than I could stand, Bethanie wrote in an e-mailed update on the cholera hospital. But when you are the manager, the final maker of decisions, the person where the buck stops, there is no time for tears.

I took the baby, and Bethanie got the IV box and prepared the site with an alcohol swab. I held the baby on my lap, her small, scraggly brown head in the crook of my arm, where I could lock it tightly if she started to squirm.

Bethanie slid the needle under the skin, but the baby made no reaction. Her brain was past the point of being bothered by the discomfort of an NG tube or the prick of a 24-gauge needle. It was dealing with bigger things, with the need to fight for the next breath.

We were still over by the card table, so there were no spectators. It was just as well, because the attempt wasn't working. The vein was too small, too flat.

"Is this a vein?" I asked, pointing to a raised area on her forehead.

Bethanie withdrew the needle from the other side.

"Hmmm. I think she just scratched herself there." She touched it lightly. "Or is it a vein?"

Bethanie slid the needle in again at the place we thought might be a vein, but there was nothing.

We returned the baby to her mother, who had come back into the hospital. She was desperate to get the NG tube out of the baby's nose, so she agreed to try one more thing: putting a needle into her tibia, the bone right below the knee.

As we gathered supplies, Bethanie explained the procedure to me.

"It's a sterile procedure, so I'll wear sterile gloves," she explained. The equipment they were using had improved since the first days of trying to turn the needle into the bone manually. In those days, not only would the needles bend, but the force needed to get the needle into the bone was so great that it was hard to suddenly let up on the pressure as soon as you were in. One time Bethanie's needle had gone entirely through the bone.

"I had my hand under the leg that time, and I felt the needle come through," she said. "It didn't break through the skin, but I knew it came through the bone. That was a very strange sensation."

Bethanie also recalled a five-year-old who had come to the hospital with eyes rolled back and sunken. He was floppy and slipping in and out of consciousness. His extremities were ice cold, and he vomited the drink he was given. Although the staff pricked him several times, no veins could be found. It was not looking good.

Bethanie decided to try going into his bone. Although nurses from the States had brought several screw-in bone needles, Bethanie had never used them and they did not come with instructions. She prepared the site, and since she was not familiar with how it was supposed to screw in, she used the pushing method instead. A crowd had gathered around the bed by this time, watching the race between the cholera and the bone needle. When the needle finally penetrated the bone with a sudden surge, there was an audible gasp and sigh of relief from the watching crowd. The boy's life was saved.

Recently, though, the hospital had received a drill specially designed for placing bone needles. It looked like a hot glue gun. We added it to our pile of supplies.

"First I'll clean the area with iodine, or whatever we have," she said.

Or whatever we have?

It was not a phrase I heard much in my experience as a student. Bethanie said it lightly, without complaint, as if she knew that we could only do as much as we could with what we had. Working in La Source, you had to be flexible.

"Then I'll numb the tissue with Lidocaine. After I have the needle in, hand me this syringe." She handed me a syringe without a needle that would lock to the top of the intraosseus (IO) needle. "I'll draw back to see if we get marrow, which will show that we are actually in the bone."

"How in the world do you know if you're in?" I asked. "What does marrow look like?"

She smiled.

"Red. Like blood. Then, if we're in, hand me this syringe with normal saline, and I'll flush the needle. Then we'll prime the tubing with more water and hook it up. We'll watch to see if it runs well, as well as watching for swelling."

She added a stabilizer to our stack, a plastic contraption to fit over the IO needle and keep it from slipping after placement.

We set up our sterile procedure right there on Bed 14. The mom held the baby on her lap, with a plastic-backed cotton pad around the baby's bottom to catch diarrhea.

Bethanie cleansed the site thoroughly and poked the Lidocaine needle into the tiny baby leg to numb the tissue. To get the most value from the numbing medicine, Bethanie twisted the needle in at different angles, pushing the Lidocaine into the widest area possible.

Again, the baby did not react at all.

"Wow, that really stings going in," Bethanie said when the baby again did not react at all. I knew that she meant, *She must not be with us.*

She connected the needle to the drill. The needle was about the same thickness as the inside shaft of a ball point pen, the part you write with.

The mother gasped and turned her face away, but the baby made no response as Bethanie pressed the power and the little drill began to whirr. It was not loud—just about the sound of a quiet sewing machine. The needle met resistance inside the skin, but then sank deeper. I thought it looked promising, but Bethanie was shaking her head.

"It's not in," she said. She waited a bit, but finally withdrew it and reached for the other knee. The wound on the first leg was minor, just a dot of red the size you would expect after withdrawing a ball point pen shaft.

"Maybe I was too far to the side," Bethanie frowned. The baby's bones were so small that it was not surprising that she had missed on the first try.

This time the needle sank into its target. Even though it was a bad thing that the baby was unresponsive, I was glad she did not need to experience the pain.

Bethanie took the syringe I had ready and drew back. A dark red, thick liquid pooled in the barrel of the syringe. She returned the marrow, flushed the needle with sterile water, and attached the IV tubing.

We were in.

When my shift ended that day, I did not feel like leaving. I was afraid that as soon as I left, the baby would die, or the father would come to take her home.

"I'll hold her again," I told Bethanie.

She frowned at me with concern.

"You need to get your rest," she said. "You're coming back on the night shift."

I held her a little longer. The mother had gone outside again, but she soon came back with some green leaves. She rubbed them over the baby's body. I assumed it was a kind of death ritual. I thought the green stuff must be herbs of some kind, but they just smelled like ordinary weeds. Around and around she rubbed them mechanically. I wondered if she really cared about this baby.

I have often tried to understand death and the dying process. Do people know when they are dying? Are they aware of their head tossing, their arms flailing? Or is that just an instinctive response of the body, reflexes from a brain that can no longer handle everything, that can no longer feel the sharp prick of a Lidocaine shot?

The baby's heart had slowed to 92 beats per minute. Normally, a slowing heart rate is a good sign, especially with cholera. A lower heart rate means the body has a good blood supply and the heart is not stressed out. However, 92 beats per minute was way too slow for this little baby. It was a sign that her body was growing tired and ready to quit. As the fluid entered her veins, however, her heart rate rose to over 100. In this case we were glad to see her heart rate increase because it meant her body was still fighting. It was incredible that such a tired little heart could find the strength to beat faster, to keep on fighting.

Eventually, I left.

Before I came back, the baby left the hospital. She died on the cycle on the way home.

Even though we think death is such a bad thing, maybe it is really like putting in a tough IV. Putting in an IV just gives a sick person even more pain, right? Yet to the people who really know what is going on, the real victory comes at the end of the pain, when the IV goes in and the person's life is saved.

I could imagine Jesus, sympathizing with the pain of the baby's death. I could even imagine Him weeping. Yet I also knew that He was the mastermind controlling the needle, knowing it was better this way. I could hear Him joyfully welcoming her to heaven with open arms and the words, "You're in!"

CHAPTER 8

MISS BALLOON
AND FRIENDS

Bless all the dear children in thy tender care . . .

After the trauma of losing the baby, the successful pediatric cases were all the more special.

I had learned how to properly say *"Bonjou"* from Joanna; I learned how to properly say *"Wi"* (yes) from a little boy with a cell phone. Although the Haitians were often out of cell phone minutes, many of them had phones.

At 6:00 one morning a ringtone pealed through the hospital. Although people had been waking up, the place had still been quiet. Not anymore.

"Bonjou!" the chubby boy answered. *"Wi!"* he said with a giant grin in his voice. Then another *"Wi!"* reverberated through the morning stillness. Each use of the word was punctuated with a giant exclamation mark.

His brother took the phone next and rattled off a more complex piece of communication.

Bethanie laughed. "He says his brother's doing fine, but he's in the hospital because he's vomiting," she explained to me.

A child was small enough to be carried in his father's arms, but occasionally even the little people came by "ambulance."

At night the ambulance of choice was a "cholera bed." People with other ailments had been carried to the clinic in beds, but the epidemic had given rise to the term "cholera bed." When I first heard the staff talk about the cholera beds, I was picturing the types of beds we sleep on in Indiana—not something you would want to carry over a mountain for two hours. These beds, however, were streamlined: a bedspring with posts at each corner and wooden poles inserted under the bed frame, extending on either side to provide handles. It was similar to how they carried the tabernacle pieces as described in the Bible.

As many as twenty or twenty-five people came along, taking turns carrying the bed as the procession crawled over the mountains along paths half the width of the bed. Where the paths were this narrow, the procession strung out single file behind the bed, usually pulling itself together like a giant worm when the path widened.

Later, back in the States, my dad questioned my story.

"How could they be carrying a bed if they also had to walk single file?" he asked.

"I don't know either," I said, "and I saw it happen."

The ambulance siren of choice was the "cholera song." To keep up their spirits and their marching rhythm, the entourage often sang the "cholera song" in time to the stamp of their feet. Of course, I did not understand the songs, but I had heard that sometimes the names "Bethanie" and "Joanna" were added to the lyrics. Sometimes, when I was not on night shift, the processions would wake me up. I would peer out my window and see them passing single file on the narrow path behind my quarters, sometimes stopping to re-arrange carriers.

If the patient was still fairly stable, the bed carriers might have taken their time and conserved their energy on the trip. Coming into the hospital, they would wait politely off to the side before explaining the situation to Bethanie in Creole. Because of the language barrier and their politeness, I sometimes did not even realize that a new patient had arrived. There was one kind of messenger, however, that could not be mistaken even with a language barrier—the men who came striding into the hospital, dripping with sweat. They went directly to a nurse, not impolite exactly, but determined to receive attention now. These were the real emergencies. Whenever this happened, I went immediately to investigate.

It was a busy evening with two cholera beds in our ambulance bay when I was sent over to the regular clinic for the second nurse. One of the new patients was another little dehydrated boy, probably about ten years old. After Bethanie and Joanna both stuck him without success, Bethanie went back to the supply cupboard for the bone needle supplies.

The "IV crowd" had gathered. Besides the staff setting up the IV, the atmosphere with the patient, family, and the rest of the hospital was pretty tense too. The ring of family members included the boy's mother.

Parents of patients coaxed and cajoled. Bethanie said that parents often threatened that the nurses would whip the children if they did not behave, or promised that the nurses would give them something if they did behave. With either promise, the parents pushed the responsibility off onto the nurse. Some parents tried to turn their child's head away. Others moaned with their child.

Whether young or old, the patient's eyes tended to follow our movements warily. The little children looked distrustfully at our array of packages, alcohol swabs, and finally the needle. The older ones knew what was coming and often looked away.

The boy cried out when Bethanie stuck him with the Lidocaine needle, twisting it this way and that in the tissue. When the little drill came out and began to whirr, the patient's mom collapsed in a moaning heap on a nearby bed. The boy continued to whimper, but I was surprised that the drilling process was not more painful.

However, when the needle was in place and Bethanie withdrew the deep red marrow, the boy's whimpers turned to screams.

"That must really kill," I said, startled. Other than childhood shots, I had never seen a procedure being done that caused the patient to scream.

"It does," Bethanie said.

He continued the piercing cries as Bethanie flushed the marrow back into the bone. As the fluid ran through the tube, into his bone marrow, and from there into the vital space of the bloodstream, the boy fell into an exhausted, whimpering silence.

"We'll want to start an IV on him before too long," Bethanie said. "To cut back on risk of infection, the bone needles should not be in place for more than twenty-four hours."

That night, pain attacked the boy. But

by this time enough fluid had been put back in that the nurses were able to get an IV into his vein. He bounced back and went home in only a few days. After patients like the baby we lost, seeing children recover and go home was exciting.

Toddlers were the worst.

"She's going to be a fighter," Bethanie predicted to me warily one hot afternoon when our clothes stuck to our bodies and the breeze refused to reach inside the hospital. The child was too young to have the self-control to endure pain silently, nor was she too sick to care. She had been in the observation tent for awhile, but when she began to vomit, Bethanie decided to admit her. Once vomiting begins, the sick are no longer able to compensate for fluid losses; therefore, vomiting was often the criterion for admission to the hospital.

Bethanie asked me to hold the little girl's arm so that she could not squirm. I settled my left arm firmly around her elbow, using my other arm to hold the headlamp close to provide extra lighting. Bethanie had found a vein in her hand. I reasoned that if I had the elbow locked, the little girl would not be able to move her forearm either.

Wrong. When Bethanie went in with the needle, the startled little girl gave a powerful jerk and began to wail. Despite her locked elbow, she pulled her hand several inches away from Bethanie, almost causing the needle to come back out. I dropped the headlight for a second, trying to save the situation.

"Which is more necessary, the light or holding her arm?" I asked hurriedly. The girl's screams were constant and loud, filling the hospital.

Bethanie's needle was not drawing any blood.

"Probably the arm," she said, pulling the needle back out. She flagged down one of her Haitian workers to come in from behind her and grasp the little girl's fingers and wrist. The toddler kept looking, unfortunately, and when she saw the needle coming again, she howled louder than ever. A small appreciative audience formed. A spirit of unity filled the hospital when there was one person screaming in pain.

"This hand is not immobilized well," Bethanie told me, taking advantage of the language barrier to voice a complaint, at the same time urging the Haitian worker to lock the little girl's fingers more completely. I also felt bad, because I knew the giant jerk at the beginning was my fault and may have cost us the IV.

Thankfully, the needle went in and the IV held. We assured the distressed little lady that we were done pricking her.

"No wonder these babies get so mad at us," I said, remembering a baby across the aisle who had fought us off whenever we tried to take her radial pulse.

"It's not surprising, is it?" Bethanie said with a sympathetic smile for the sniffling little girl.

A few hours later I got the chance to blow up a balloon for her. I did not know if she would even let me get close, but she had actually calmed down enough to choose which color balloon she wanted. Her mother made sure she said *"Mèsi."*

Usually we dangled the balloons with ribbon over the child's bed. I hung it right above the middle of her bed where she could easily see it.

A few minutes later she began swatting the balloon, grinning broadly as it swung away from her and then came back to be hit again. Maybe she was imagining that the balloon was a nurse; it was hard to tell. Whatever the case, she would watch the balloon coming closer and closer, waiting until it was right beside her, before giving it another terrific swat. This child did everything in life with force, whether screaming or hitting a balloon.

"I'm sure glad we didn't have to stick her more than that," Bethanie said with relief. There would be no smoothing over pain with this child. She noticed everything.

Little Miss Balloon was on the road to recovery by evening and captured the attention of the hospital with her chatter. She entertained her fellow patients and their caretakers by jabbering about a "man who hurt his eyes."

In the middle of the night, it happened. Her IV went bad.

The entire hospital woke up to the tune of her screaming as the night nurses stuck her veins fruitlessly. They finally gave up and got out the bone-drilling equipment.

Bethanie told the mother to be careful not to allow her daughter to thrash her limbs with the needle in her leg. "It's like trying to take a snake to church to keep her still," the mother worried.

Like the baby we had lost, the first knee did not work. Finally the needle was lodged in the second tibia, with the IV fluid dripping.

About half an hour later the night shift saw that the knee was swelling. The fluid was not going into the bone.

"Well, there's nothing left except the femur," Bethanie said.

They started the whole process over again, drilling into the child's leg just below the hip joint. Again, the first one did not work. Finally, with the fourth Lidocaine shot and the fourth whirr of the drill, the needle was lodged in the one remaining bone.

When I came on for the morning shift, I could not believe the story. Not only that, but the child's upper leg was beginning to swell.

Fortunately, Miss Balloon was no longer losing much fluid. When the bone needle came out, we decided to try her on oral fluids.

When she wasn't screaming in pain, she sat on her bed as though she owned the world and beamed at everyone. She seemed to be smart enough to realize that as long as the nurses did not have sharps in their hands, they were safe and might even bring her a balloon. She had the cutest little cough that came out in an opinionated sort of way. At night I saw her huddled under the same sheet as her mother. She spoke just as loudly as she pleased, not regarding the other twenty people trying to sleep. Her mother answered more quietly, in a sample tone of the voice she would recommend under the circumstances.

Besides telling the little girl to say *"Mèsi"* for the balloon, her mother washed her own sheets and spread them out on a tree to dry with the devotion of a dedicated cleaner. She dressed herself with a matching blue headdress and blue dress. Her care for her child and herself was encouraging to see. It was easy to believe that her child would continue to receive good care at home.

It was so fun to see the little ones go home, fully recovered.

CHAPTER 9

THE FIFTEEN-SECOND JOB

All is calm, all is bright . . .

Holding sick babies and watching toddlers recover, grin at us, and play with their balloons was exciting. Landing a successful IV or IO into a severely dehydrated patient was the crowning part of our duties. But much of our time was spent on more tedious tasks that were not all that exciting, yet very necessary.

Did some people just naturally vomit loudly, or did they actually have the disease that much worse? I never knew.

"That might be your background noise for the night," one of the staff laughed when I arrived for night shift one evening. The man in Bed 21 had just arrived. He wore a black T-shirt that said "Ted's Kickin' Chicken" on the back, and was vomiting so loudly that the people outside the hospital had been imitating him. His vomiting came without warning and with great force. At least he was hitting the bucket. Severe patients sometimes projected vomit onto the floor, across the room, or even onto a staff member.

The good thing was that the vomit and diarrhea were really not that gross. With the small intestine draining the body, both the vomit and diarrhea were just water. However, the vomiting looked painful, with its victims hanging over their buckets and bringing up mouthful after mouthful with violent retches, sometimes vomiting a liter at a time in one steady, forceful torrent.

Sometimes worms were involved. If we found a worm on a pillow or in a toileting bucket, we put a special sticky note on their chart: DEWORM ON DISCHARGE.

I went to take Bed 21's blood pressure for 10:00 rounds as the hospital was beginning to settle down for the night. I had the blood pressure cuff wrapped around his upper arm when he suddenly reared up on that arm. In the same moment his wife snatched the bucket and held it up for him, and I leaped back without my equipment as the water began to gush. I escaped with only a light mist, but I went immediately to the hand sanitizer and generously cleaned my arms while Bed 21 finished his vomiting spell.

We used the same equipment on everyone, which seemed awful. The truth was though, that the patients in the hospital were at less risk from this than we were, because they already had the same disease.

Taking vital signs at night was probably my least favorite job. Even though it was an important safeguard to take blood pressures and pulses every two hours, I hated waking people up five times a night.

In nursing school they taught us to start with the least invasive or least painful procedure first. Remembering this, I developed a streamlined nighttime ritual. I gathered my equipment, trying to make a little noise in the hope that some people would wake up on their own. It usually didn't work.

If the patients were sleeping, I tapped them lightly on the

arm, tugged at their blankets, or spoke softly: "Just have to take your blood pressure real quick." Of course I was speaking English and they did not understand me, but I always hoped my tone of voice would be soothing enough to wake them gently out of sleep. If the arm I needed (the one without the IV) was on the inside of the bed where I couldn't reach easily, I would often crawl up on the bed so they would not have to move as far.

As soon as I could, even if the person was still sleeping, I would slip a few fingers lightly on that magic groove on the inside of the wrist right in line with the thumb, where you can almost always find a pulse. My hope was that when I counted their pulse for fifteen seconds, they would wake up enough to realize that I was going to take their blood pressure next, and lay their arm out nicely for me. Again, this usually did not work.

Some patients would sleepily pull their arm back into the warmth of their sheet. Others would clench their arm tightly and you could hardly budge it in the first place. Still others would allow you to start taking the pressure, but would wiggle their arm and make it hard to hear the beating through your stethoscope.

"*Pa souke!*" I would say with a desperate appeal to my lousy Creole. If I had to redo the pressure, I would shake my head sadly and say "*Ankò*" (again), one of the few other Creole words in my vocabulary.

There were a few wonderful patients, like Number 16, who had been in the hospital for a few days, learned the routine, and helped us out. He was a young man and had a sheet with giant orange blocks like an oversized gingham tablecloth. At night he would wrap himself from head to toe like a mummy, as my younger brother used to do on the living room floor with a throw. As soon as Number 16 heard me coming close with my equipment, he would find a slit in his burial wraps, push his right arm through (he knew we needed the one without the IV), and extend it for the blood pressure cuff. With such perfect conditions, I took his pulse and blood pressure in record time, and the arm disappeared as smoothly as it had come.

My watch was one of the most familiar faces to me on those shifts. Not only did we measure the pulses for fifteen seconds, but we also measured drip rates for fifteen seconds. Back in nursing school I sometimes had trouble remembering which number I had started the second hand on, but this weakness dissolved after hundreds of measurements. If I started counting when the second hand was at the 7, I would be done at the 10. If I started at the 4, I was done at the 7. My mental clock became so trained that I think I could have recorded fairly accurate pulses without a time piece.

Because we were counting for a quarter of a minute, we learned the multiples of four. If a person has 17 beats in 15 seconds, how many does he have in a minute? 68. 19=76, 23=92.

Keeping the IV bags running was a tedious chore as well. If you let a bag run out, bad things could happen. The worst possibility was that the catheter would clot off because there was no flow. If a line seemed to be blocked or was dripping slowly, we would try to flush it with a syringe of normal saline. If it would not flush, Joanna showed me how to take apart the IV line and try to flush directly through the port of the catheter. If this still did not help, the catheter would have to be taken out and a new IV started. As a student who had not worked with IVs much, I was pleased to be able to pick up some new skills, but it was still a bother at 4 a.m.

The other bothersome thing that happened if we let a bag run dry was that the tubing would fill with air. I learned to clamp off the lower line and inject normal saline into the rubber port with a needle. This fluid pushed the air up the line and out into the drip chamber at the top, keeping the patient from getting a dose of air in the veins.

Ironically, the fewer bags we had hanging, the easier it seemed to miss one. The number of patients at the hospital peaked during Ethan and Anna's first week. Anna reported that on one of her first night shifts, she had twenty-seven IV bags to watch and change, and she did not think she had missed any of them. She did have help, however. During the busiest days and nights, some of the non-medical missionary staff came to help. Steve and one of the pastors, Paul, helped out on day shifts, watching IV bags, recording vital signs, and helping with crowd control. Nelson and the other pastor, Matt, assisted on night shifts.

Bed 21, whose noisy vomiting eventually eased off, became one of my favorite patients. I liked his spirit, the energy for life hidden under "Ted's Kickin' Chicken." It took him days to recover from his more severe case, but eventually he gained full recovery. He would have died without treatment, I was certain.

CHAPTER 10

NUMBER 9

Sorrow and grief are lulled by thy light . . .

Bethanie had warned me that there could be a praise and worship service in the middle of the night, but it still came as a bit of a shock when the hospital gradually awoke and one by one joined in a high-volume song that must have been heard for miles around.

The leader of the service was a tall man who had been at the hospital as a caretaker for some time and had apparently developed feelings of ownership. He often wore a too large sweater printed with the words "Beverly Hills Polo Club."

The sweater made an impression on me in several ways. First, Haiti was full of men wearing shirts that were too large. I could only conclude that they were wearing clothes handed down to them from their better-fed brothers to the northwest. Second, the words "Beverly Hills Polo Club" created an image of wealth, leisure, and California sunshine in my mind that contrasted starkly with the tall, authoritative man who lived on Haiti's rough, windblown hillsides and led loud singing in a tarp hospital at 2 a.m.

The Beverly Hills man felt ownership at the hospital because he had been there for so long. Occasionally he exercised this authority over other patients.

"You must drink!" he told a little tyke one time, forcing the oral rehydration solution into the child's mouth. A moment later the child vomited directly on him.

For all his bossiness, however, his worship service was contagious. Half asleep, the people joined the song, their mouths moving as they lay flat on their backs. Voices harmonized with special parts. Random arms extended into the air as the people praised the Lord or sleepily kept time to the beat. Even I, the surprised American nursing student charting vital signs at the card table nurses' station, found a lonely beauty in the haunting chords that rose and fell with lilting repetition during the dark night.

Bethanie woke up during the clamor and came out to the main room shaking her head with dismay at the destruction of her few precious hours of sleep. She made a lap or two through the aisles of beds, checking the most critical patients. I had noticed that she had an uncanny sense of which patient to keep in mind. In the middle of the night, she would wake from a dead sleep in her nest of blankets on the floor and say, "How is 18's blood pressure?"

In the still hours of the night, after the singing and praying had ceased, I ran into my first real frustration. I had failed to replace one of the bags in time to keep air out of the line, so I was trying to flush it back. The groggy patient, however, was sitting forward on her bed, making it almost impossible for me to reach the roller clamp while pinching the lower line and inserting the needle into the rubber port. I tried several strategies, including using English and hand motions to try to get the woman to scoot back. *What they don't teach you in nursing school,* was all I could think as I crouched on the patient's bed. I finally solved my problem of an insufficient number of hands by uncapping the needle with my teeth.

When I finally managed to force the air out of the line and turn the roller clamp open, the fluid refused to drip. I drew more normal saline into a new syringe, clamped off the upper line, and tried to flush the catheter. It refused to flush, probably having clotted off.

As much as I hated to wake Bethanie again, I had no choice now. I could not put in a new IV by myself. Earlier that day I had put one in with Anna's assistance, but I had gotten blood everywhere. I certainly was not ready to do one on my own.

With her skill of sudden wakefulness, Bethanie jerked awake instantly. I was showing her the IV site, when we looked across the aisle. The patient in Bed 11 was sitting on the foot of his bed, looking disoriented, with the IV line stretched nearly taut to the bag. Something was not right.

Earlier in the day he had seemed confused and fought us when we needed to take his blood pressure. "He wasn't like this when he came in?" I asked.

"No, he wasn't."

Now with the help of his groggy wife and some rapid Creole, Bethanie powered the confused man back to his pillow.

"I wonder why he's breathing like that," she said.

"I was trying to remember if it was a change for him or not," I said. I had heard it and knew it was not good.

"I don't remember hearing it before," she said. The rapid, labored respirations held a chilling resemblance to the breathing of the woman who had died the night before a few beds down the row. Bethanie suspected that she had other issues . . . renal failure, maybe. But what if the same thing that had killed her was now striking Number 11?

When we reported off that morning, Bethanie shared that she was uneasy about the IV fluids we were using.

"We were using lactated Ringer's solution," she said. "Then our supplier said he couldn't find any lactated Ringer's for us, but that a regular Ringer's solution was available."

Lactated Ringer's, a commonly used IV solution, not only provides fluid replacement, but also supplies electrolytes: sodium, potassium, chloride, and calcium. The Ringer's solution the hospital was now using contained the same electrolytes, but in slightly differing amounts. Also, the lactated Ringer's solution contained lactate, while the other solution did not. Lactate, although it is an acid, actually helps keep the body from accumulating too much acid.

The kidneys are normally in charge of protecting the delicate balance between acids and bases in the body. However, sometimes the kidneys become overwhelmed and the acid builds up, creating a potentially deadly condition called acidosis. People with severe diarrhea, kidney failure, or undiagnosed Type 1 diabetes are all at risk for acidosis.

The lungs are the next organ to come in as backup, because they control carbon dioxide levels. Carbon dioxide is also an acid. The lungs sense the rising acid levels and come on board, trying to blow off extra carbon dioxide. This creates a very distinct, heavy breathing pattern.

When I came back on that evening for the 4–9 shift, Number 11 had become Number 9. The sun shone much hotter on the Bed 11 side of the hospital, so they had moved him over to the shade, trying to make him more comfortable. The man was restless and tossing, throwing back his head and exhaling long and noisily.

Bethanie was sure by now that he had acidosis. Joanna agreed.

"He reminds me a lot of some of the diabetic patients I used to take care of who had acidosis," she said.

I, too, had heard breathing like this before. It always filled me with sadness to listen to the desperate attempt of the lungs to try to save the body and other organs. Further, in my experience, this kind of breathing had been one of the trademarks of a losing battle.

CHAPTER 11

NO INFORMATION

While around us the dark billows roll . . .

"I wonder if there's something more we could do," Bethanie said, shaking her head. "I just have the one book that mentions metabolic acidosis, and it doesn't say much." Bethanie had a number of medical reference books on her shelves, but this was the book of choice for this situation because it discussed metabolic acidosis.

I looked at *Merck's Manual of Medical Care, Home Edition.* If the idea of a hospital being unable to access lactated Ringer's solution had been shocking to me, this was more so. Coming from a world of Google, college libraries, and people overrun with too much information, the idea of not being able to access reference information was as foreign to me as the donkeys on the path or the *pitimi* (sorghum or millet) bobbing against the blue sky.

"I wonder if we could give him baking soda?" she mused again. "Baking soda is a base, so it should help to neutralize all that acid."

"Do you have any resource people you could contact?" I asked.

"Not really," she said. "My brother is a doctor, but he's a surgeon. My cousin is a doctor, but she's a pediatrician."

Bethanie bent thoughtfully over *Merck's Manual* as we both listened to the man's lungs trying to save his body, but sounding tired.

Anna, who was still finishing up some charting from her shift, overheard our conversation.

"Do you mind if I call someone?" she asked. She knew a doctor personally who was a general family practitioner.

"Sure, go ahead," Bethanie said. They discussed which phone she should use. Of course, we were not using the trusty Sprint and Verizon phones we had brought with us.

"If he tells us to use baking soda, we have some up at our house in the cupboard above the stove," Bethanie told her as she left.

My experience with acidosis went back to the pet calf I had in my childhood. My father, a veterinarian, had used a baking soda and water mixture to try to save my calf's life. We used a glass soda bottle (the only one we could find was a 1979 7-Up bottle he had saved from college) to force the fluid down the throat of the uncooperative calf. It had died anyway.

As if the evening shift were not complex enough already, another situation arose while Anna was gone to contact the doctor. There was someone new who needed attention in the observation tent.

It was about 5:00, so the tent was still lit with sunlight, but the harsh heat was gone. A man sat on the bench inside the tent, holding a four-year-old girl across his knees. The crowd who had come with the child and was now peering under the tent flap was so densely packed that it seemed to be only a bouquet of brown faces with no necks. While Bethanie conversed in Creole and assessed the child, I counted her respirations: 44 breaths per minute. Her eyes were closed and her body lay limply in her father's arms.

Bethanie turned to me with the translation. The child did not have cholera.

"They say she drank a lot of alcohol this morning at 8:00, and now she is like this. I don't know what we can do for her. It's been so long that the alcohol is in her bloodstream by now."

More conversation in Creole, with input from some of the faces in the opening. One must have been the child's mother, but I had given up trying to distinguish family relationships when such a big crowd came. Bethanie explained to the people that it would not be wise to bring the child into the cholera hospital since she did not have cholera.

"I don't know if it would help to put an IV in her," Bethanie said to me. "I guess we can look it up and see if there is anything to do for her."

"Narcan?" I asked. Recalling the pages of my nursing textbook, I remembered the antidote for sedation-producing drugs like alcohol.

"Probably," Bethanie said. From her tone of voice I knew we did not have Narcan on hand. "If they would have come sooner, we could have done a gastric lavage to clean out her stomach or something," she said. "But it's been too long."

Other than recommending Narcan, *Merck's* did not help much for this patient either. Bethanie decided to put an IV in her anyway. It couldn't hurt.

Anna returned with her usual energy—and instructions from her doctor friend. He had done a bit of quick research and had suggested a baking soda and water formula to be taken by mouth, or, if the patient could not swallow, by nasogastric tube. With as much discomfort as the man was in, I hoped we would not have to put a tube into his nose and down into his stomach. Although I wanted to do everything possible for him, my instinct told me that the man was dying.

"My doctor friend did say that we could give it through IV if we had a way of sterilizing the baking soda," Anna said, but Bethanie agreed that giving it by mouth was a better option.

While Anna prepared the baking soda mixture, Bethanie went outside to start the IV on the little girl. She talked to the family honestly, telling them that she did not know if it would help.

Steve had come down to the hospital, as he often did. With his help Bethanie put in the IV. While she slipped back into the hospital to assist with Number 9, Steve taped the IV in place and hung the bag of fluid above the little girl. Using the stethoscope Bethanie had left, he monitored her breathing and heart beat. The respirations were regular but rapid, and her heart rate was racing as well.

Inside, Anna stirred the baking soda mixture in one of the plastic cups we used to give drinks of oral rehydration solution and offered it to the man in Bed 9. Even between the two of us, it was hopeless. By this time, besides the tossing and restlessness, his entire body was stiff, and we could barely get him to bend at the waist. The baking soda mixture spilled into his mouth and out again at the corners. He choked and retched and fought the cup. It was hard to tell if it was really the man himself fighting, or if it was just a reaction from a frustrated body.

While Anna quickly measured the stomach tube to fit the

man, I helped support him in an upright position. I had been taught that a patient should swallow while a stomach tube was being inserted through the nose and down the esophagus. The water swallowing helped open the esophagus and prevent the thin plastic tube from going down the trachea into the lungs. But this man obviously was not going to swallow for us.

"Well, I've been told that tipping the chin forward has the same effect," Anna said.

Even tipping the chin looked like a major task with this man, who was stiff, restless, breathing with effort, and combative. The man choked and struggled as we cranked his head forward and Anna threaded the tube through his nose. Bethanie came in from the observation tent and helped us. Anna got the tube in quickly and smoothly, landing it in the stomach. Bethanie helped to draw up the baking soda mixture into a large syringe and feed it through the tube. Anna taped the tube to the man's nose to keep it from slipping.

I avoided the faces of his wife and the other caretakers. Watching an NG tube being put in is not pretty no matter who the patient is, but it has to be worse if it is your husband, brother, dad, or close friend. And, like me, the family had given up hope. They had called for a bed to be sent for the man so that he could go home to die instead of dying in the hospital. But the bed had not arrived yet, and as long as he was in the hospital, we felt responsible to try everything we could.

Maybe I'm just cynical, I thought. My private home health client with a brain tumor had died with this breathing pattern. My childhood calf had died the same way, despite having baking soda channeled to its stomach. That did not mean that everyone like this would have to die. While there is life there is hope, right?

The scene I was really reliving had nothing to do with a client or my childhood. Almost exactly five months before, I had been crouching with my family in our living room as my own mother breathed heavily and tossed restlessly on her hospital bed. As the morning turned to afternoon, and the afternoon turned to night, we watched on, singing sometimes, speaking to her sometimes. Over everything, the sound of her breathing was heard. Finally, as the sunset faded to blackness, her breathing grew lighter and lighter, and an expression of peace replaced the look of tension and the movements of restlessness. At 9:25 p.m. she took her last breath.

I had too much experience with labored breathing.

CHAPTER 12

DEATH

Thou hope of each mortal in death's lonely night . . .

Darkness was falling over La Source like a curtain. We switched on our light bulbs embedded in the wooden rafters above every other bed. Number 9's breathing filled the room, making everyone in the hospital quiet and thoughtful.

We were in the middle of putting in the NG tube and the baking soda when Steve came in for Bethanie.

"I think we're losing her," he said, referring to the alcohol overdose case. Only a few minutes after Bethanie left, Steve had noticed the child's breathing becoming shallow and less frequent.

"I'll be out as soon as we're done," Bethanie promised, "but I don't think there's anything else to do."

By the time Steve returned, the little girl was gasping her last breaths.

"*L'ap kite nou*" (She's leaving us), Steve said to the uncle who was holding her. He bent his head over her mouth, cupping his hand between her mouth and his ear.

I followed Bethanie out to the observation tent when we finished with Number 9. Steve was moving the stethoscope over the little girl's chest, listening.

"Just to make sure," I heard him say.

The din began after Bethanie pronounced her dead. As Steve said later, several of the little girl's aunts "dissolved into a frenzied agony." A crowd of several dozen milled beside the hospital, wailing and crying. At least two of the aunts passed out.

Inside the blue building, glowing in the night, Number 9 breathed noisily.

Even the staff grew somber. Two deaths in the last few days, with a third death threatening. We gathered around the card table nurses' station.

If they had just brought the little girl in sooner. She was a case that could have been saved.

I ventured to say that I was confused by the little girl's rapid breathing.

"I thought people with overdoses like that breathe slowly," I said.

"She did breathe less and less at the end," Steve said.

It was hard to tell by the light of a few light bulbs, but I wondered if his eyes were red. I remembered him saying, "Just to make sure." The little girl was the same age as his son, and I knew he had been reluctant to announce that she had died.

My own emotional tension ran high. As I filled in vital signs on our paper card charts, the people in the hospital began to sing. A circle of people placed their hands on Number 9, the Beverly Hills Polo Club man in their midst. I kept on writing down numbers, but Bethanie paused for a minute. She leaned back in her folding chair, watching, humming along with the song. She was at home here.

My mind turned to home that night. Although Christmas would never be the same without Mom, I did not feel that

I was "running away" by going to Haiti over the holidays. I had just felt that going to Haiti to work in a cholera hospital would be a good end to a tough year. Now it was the night after Christmas, and I was revisiting scenes from home while thousands of miles away.

The bed to take the man home finally arrived a little before nine. Ethan had already come down to take my place, and when we heard the bed coming, we went out together to see if it was a new patient.

Despite the stamping, singing, and flare, this bed was empty. Inside the blue glow, Number 9's breaths had diminished to slow puffs.

"I think we're losing him," Bethanie said.

Foam gathered at the corners of his mouth. A friend or relative rubbed the man's chest with soap. His breaths came slower and slower. Four breaths a minute.

Ethan, who worked in a nursing home, said that sometimes it took days for an old person to die, even after they were breathing that slowly. But I felt certain it could not go on long in this case. For one thing, this was not an old man.

The man's wife left the room, weeping, with another younger woman following her with a hand on her shoulder. Would another mourning party develop? The crowd wailing over the little girl had dispersed, leaving an uneasy silence. Even the noisy breathing from Number 9 had quieted.

I felt irresistibly drawn to watch at the bedside. I stood with my watch, counting the respirations.

"Katrina, can you help me?" Bethanie asked. She was lugging a heavy roll of gray tarp from a back corner of the supply room. Together we unrolled it enough to cut off a piece big enough to wrap the man's body. As I folded the piece and trimmed off an extra corner, Bethanie gave instructions to a group of men, probably the ones who had come with the empty bed. She stood in front of them, half their size, with a bottle of Clorox and a lump of cotton. As she talked, she pulled off pieces of the cotton. They listened to her instructions quietly and took the Clorox and cotton from her. Then they took the folded piece of tarp from me.

I slipped away and watched the man for several full minutes. There were no breaths.

"I'm pretty sure he's gone," I told Bethanie. After finishing her instructions to the men, she explained to Ethan and me that to keep the cholera from spreading, the bodies were wrapped in the tarp. Clorox-saturated cotton pieces were put into the corpse's nose, mouth, ears, and rectum to prevent the escape of body fluids, which could wash into a river after a rain.

"I'll help them take care of the body," Bethanie said, moving to the bedside.

Sitting at the card table on our folding chairs, Ethan and I talked about death. When Bethanie returned, she asked what we were talking about.

"I was just saying that Number 9's death was similar to my mom's death. She died this summer."

It is odd how people vary in their response to death. When you tell someone that your mom died recently, a lot of people will shut up. They do not know what to say, and they are afraid to say the wrong thing. I don't blame them. Grieving people are a mess.

But overall, the most sensitive and understanding people will ask at least a few questions, giving the grieving person a door to open and talk through if they want to, or else to slam shut if the timing and mood are not right. Because people want to be understanding, they are willing to take the risk of getting the slammed door.

I was not surprised that Bethanie took the risk, asking me several times in the next days about my mom's death. I told her some bare details, but I was not really in the mood to say much.

I did admit to her that it was one of the things that had brought me to Haiti. Somehow, I felt the time at the cholera hospital would be a good way to spend the holidays. I did not know why.

It had been a long day. Bethanie wrapped herself up on the cement floor and went to sleep, and I left the night shift to Ethan.

CHAPTER 13

MOUNTAIN CLIMB

Oh beautiful star, the hope of rest . . .

In the days between Christmas and New Year, the patient load had dropped to a remarkable low. Bethanie consented to cover one shift so that all three volunteer nurses (Ethan, Anna, and I at the time) could be off at the same time to climb the mountain that rose behind the hospital. We set off up the trail with two young Haitian guides. Steve had also pointed us in the right direction and showed us where we would end up.

I thought of my mom several times on that climb. For one thing, I was thinking of Moses in the Bible, climbing the mountain to see over to a land he was not allowed to enter because of his one disobedience. I wondered why God had not allowed him to enter the land, when he had spent so many years serving Him. Was it not almost worse to be able to see it and imagine all the children of Israel going in without him, finally able to arrive in the land of milk and honey?

Yet, despite the questions, I knew that God had treated Moses with incredible care. Moses had seen God. Moses showed up on the Mount of Transfiguration and in the book of Hebrews. He is known as the meekest man on earth. Most comforting to me, God Himself had buried his old and tired body. There can be no question that, despite not letting Moses live to be with his people when they entered Canaan, God thought of him as one of His greatest leaders.

So, just because God had not allowed my mother to live to see her grandchildren or attend family weddings or graduations, was that proof that He had not used her life in powerful ways? No. Maybe God has a special attachment to people who have been denied something they greatly desired. Maybe the rewards my mom was experiencing at the very moment that I was climbing the mountain more than made up for the fact that her body aged forty years in four months.

I wondered if it was possible for her to know that I was here in Haiti taking care of sick people and climbing mountains with new friends whom I had learned to appreciate in just a few days.

Several times on the way up we stopped to turn around and look at the awesome view behind us. Maybe sometimes we were pretending to stop for the view while actually stopping to catch our breath. Regardless of the reason, allowing our eyes to feast on the sights was worthwhile. We could see the ocean, a shimmery gray-green background to the rockiness of the scenery. We saw where a river emptied into the ocean.

"There's a word for that," I said, pointing out the junction of the river and ocean. "I can't think of it . . ."

"You're right," Anna said. "It's not a strait . . ."

"Almost like a delta, but not . . ." I mused.

"My mom would know it," Anna said.

My mom was good with words too, I thought instinctively.

"Try calling her," Ethan said to Anna, laughing, because

of course our cell phones didn't work. "You probably have service up here."

Am I closer to being able to communicate to my mom too? I wondered. It seemed possible; we were so close to the sky, so uncluttered with life, standing on a mountain path up here in northern Haiti.

It was almost dark when we reached the top. We took a fun photo of our group with our arms pumped in triumph. Climbing that mountain was quite an achievement. That is, it was quite an achievement if you did not compare yourself to the other people on the mountain path. There was a man climbing up the path with a full five-gallon bucket on one shoulder, two sheep on a leash, and two more sheep trailing along behind. Another man was carrying a huge sack on his head while directing a heavily laden donkey. We also remembered that Bethanie had reported to us that she had climbed the mountain with friends once in forty-five minutes, probably half the time it took us.

For foreigners, though, it was not bad. We descended much more quickly, helped by the light of a flashlight and Anna's cell phone. We entertained ourselves by quoting poetry. Anna and I laughed with each other again, because we knew a number of the same poems by heart. As we quoted Robert Frost's "The Road Not Taken" together, it seemed to apply very much to us. Going to Haiti over Christmas was definitely the "road less traveled by."

> *Oh, I kept the first for another day!*
> *Yet knowing how way leads on to way,*
> *I doubted if I should ever come back.*

Two roads diverged in a wood, and I—
I took the one less traveled by,
And that has made all the difference.[1]

Anna quoted the entire "Go Down, Death" by James Weldon Johnson, a lengthy piece that once again took me back to the living room of my parents' home and the long days of last summer. Death is a horrible thing to wait for. Yet the poem, set in the Deep South, made death sound like a simple change of position.

And Death took her up like a baby,
And she lay in his icy arms,
But she didn't feel no chill.[2]

At the bottom of the mountain, we paid our guides with American dollars and bouncy balls, and retired to the nurses' house. We ate supper, tasted goat, and played a lively game of Qwirkle, the new game Anna had brought along. We reveled in the leisure time, laughing, talking, and trying to skip Anna's turn, until Ethan had to leave for the night shift.

---

[1] Frost, Robert, *Mountain Interval,* New York: Henry Holt and Company, 1920; Bartleby.com, 1999. www.bartleby.com/119/. Accessed on February 24, 2011.

[2] From *God's Trombones* by James Weldon Johnson. Copyright © 1927 The Viking Press, Inc., renewed 1955 by Grace Nail Johnson. Used by permission of Viking Penguin, a division of Penguin Books USA Inc. http://www.poets.org/viewmedia.php/prmMID/15586. Accessed on February 24, 2011.

CHAPTER 14

QUESTION OF LOYALTY

No more let sins and sorrows grow . . .

Most patients were well cared for by their family members. The caretakers helped the patients wash up, brought their food, and made them comfortable at night. If we had empty beds, the family members often stretched out themselves.

One morning Ethan made it to the end of the night shift and still had creativity and energy to spare. He selected a young caretaker at the head of the room who was sleeping soundly on a bed close to the nurses' station. He pulled a large, needled syringe from the supply shelves, got the attention of the rest of the hospital (most of whom were awake), and positioned the syringe just right, ready to plunge into the visitor. Then he woke him up.

"No! No! No!" the young man shouted as the rest of the spectators howled. Ethan was still chuckling when he told the story.

The "spectators" tended to laugh at a lot of things, we found. Anna received a chorus of laughter when she screeched at a cricket that would not release its grip on her. We non-Creole speakers were probably the preferred recipients of laughter because we could be discussed without understanding what was being said.

But they also laughed at each other.

Once, a young man with abdominal pain and vomiting was admitted to the clinic. He spent most of the day sharing his pain with the world.

"*M'ap mouri, m'ap mouri, m'ap mouri!*" (I'm dying!)

"Oh, my stomach oooooooo! Oh, my stomach ooooooooo! Oh, my stomach ooooooooo!"

He varied these outbursts with occasional requests.

"Nurse, can't you get me something to help me sleep?"

"Please rub my belly!" (The nurses left that task up to the family members.)

"Can't you do an X-ray?"

The broadcast usually grew worse and worse until there was a sudden burst of projectile vomiting. With the pain somewhat relieved, he would then relax for a bit. As the pressure built up again, he started all over.

"Oh, my stomach ooooooo!"

The nurses were all glad when he could be discharged the next day. However, the next few nights the remaining patients imitated him, punctuating the moaning and groaning with hysterical fits of laughter.

The time I felt most annoyed was the night I was taking care of the mentally handicapped lady. She had no caretakers. Maybe her family did not want to care for her because of her handicap. For whatever reason, I was primary caregiver that night.

It was a long night. She had lots of diarrhea. She almost never hit the bucket.

Early in the evening I gloved up and armed myself with supplies: fresh cardboard to slip under the woman and paper towels to clean up the mess. I was greeted with the jeers of several fun-loving ladies.

"Are you laughing at me?" I asked, more out of curiosity than anger. They couldn't understand me anyway.

Bethanie frowned and spoke to them in Creole.

"I think they are laughing more at the lady for being such a mess than at you," she said.

Not only should the family have stayed to take care of the lady, but they also should have been there to supply her with clothes and blankets. Several times during the night I found her soaked in her own bed clothes. I knew our supply of sheets was small, but I finally dipped into the supply room and brought her one. I covered her with a nice dry sheet and hoped things would improve.

Sadly, the dry sheet did not stay dry for long. It was true that the diarrhea did not have much odor, but it was so thin and watery that it soaked up all the linen . . . again. I tried to ignore the whole beans and seeds that had been rushed through her intestines unprocessed. I do not consider myself to be the gagging kind, but I almost vomited that night.

While the whole night was frustrating to me, I also felt sorry for her. She shivered in a curled heap under the linens, which kept getting soaked all over again.

The next day Joanna got the ingenious idea to dress her in a surgical gown. They also cleaned her up and managed to position her over the hole. When I came on duty again, she was warm and dry and resting comfortably.

But if I thought I had it bad, Joanna's story from the early years of the clinic corrected my attitude.

The man's name was Sèntàn, and he had leprosy (Hansen's disease). His family did not want to care for him, and he did a poor job of taking his medicine. Time after time Sèntàn came to the clinic with sores on his hands and feet. His fingers disappeared. Finally, Joanna took the desperate case to a hospital, but here again he would not comply with instructions, or perhaps was simply unable to take his medicine.

In her eleven years of nursing practice in Haiti, Joanna says she has never seen such a pathetic situation. The family treated Sèntàn like dirt.

"When you die, we will just throw your skeleton in the ravine," his stepfather told him.

The disease progressed. Sèntàn became bedfast and developed a large, ulcerous bed sore on his tailbone. The rest of his body was also covered with sores. The family continued to ignore him.

I finally decided it doesn't do any good to ask the family to keep him clean if I am not willing to do it myself, Joanna writes.

As Sèntàn's death neared, Joanna went to his house every week to give him a bath. He developed profuse diarrhea. Each time she went, his sheets were soaked with stool and drainage from his sores. Flies swarmed his body.

I could not stand the thought of him dying and not be ready to meet his Maker, Joanna shares. *I prayed that God would take him when he is ready to meet his Maker.*

Joanna struggled to understand why God would let the poor man linger when he was suffering so much, yet she continued to pray for his salvation. Sèntàn was also very troubled about his stepfather's comment about the ravine. One of the mission staff promised to provide a nice burial for him.

The last time Joanna went to bathe his ravaged body, her brother Bobby went with her. Bobby asked Sèntàn about his salvation. Then, while Joanna bathed him, they both sang songs.

He was in excruciating pain and had a high fever. He was skin and bones and was deathly ill, but in spite of all that he joined us in singing, and he sang with all his might with a very lusty voice. I can still hear him, Joanna remembers.

He died the following night.

CHAPTER 15

NO QUESTION
OF LOYALTY

He comes to make His blessings known . . .

It was not a great day to find no radial pulse.

New Year's Day may be a holiday in many countries, but in Haiti, it is *the* holiday. This is partly because New Year's Day is also Independence Day for Haiti. Spain, England, and France had all occupied Haiti at various times, until Haiti became independent from France on January 1, 1804.

This history explains the Creole language. Creole is a combination of French, English, and Spanish, with a higher percentage of French, and a few African words mixed in.

Prior to New Year's Day, Haitians whitewash their houses and launder their sheets. They clean their houses thoroughly, taking everything out into the yard. In a tradition perhaps more practical than the one in the States, people see the New Year in by getting up to watch the sun rise.

The church at La Source had a 4 a.m. service. Songs floated up to the hospital where I was working night shift in the blue glow.

People give each other gifts and have parties. Everyone makes and shares pumpkin soup.

"So what do I have to do to get to taste some pumpkin soup?" I asked Bethanie.

"Just be around," she said.

I was, and I got some. I actually ate it at the kitchen table in the nurses' house. The pumpkin itself was pureed into a wonderful thick broth. Other root vegetables were cooked in it, such as cassava, potatoes, onions, and carrots. People often included noodles or spaghetti in the New Year's Day pumpkin soup.

Joanna told me that morning that she suspected no one would come to the hospital on such a holiday unless they were quite ill.

I was down for the evening shift from 4:00 to 9:00.

"That might be one for us," Joanna said when she heard a cycle outside. "It pulled up and stopped."

By the time I made my way to the other end of the hospital and through the observation tent, Steve and another man were helping a young woman from the cycle. I guessed her to be in her mid-twenties. I took her wrist to check for her radial pulse, always our first diagnostic test for rating the severity of cholera.

"I'm not getting anything, are you?" Steve asked, and I saw that he was testing the woman's other wrist.

"No."

Her entire forearm was cold. When we had settled her in Bed 4, Joanna told me I could take a look at her veins while she changed an IV bag. I slipped our slender blue tourniquet around her upper arm and ran the tips of my fingers along her arm.

"Joanna," I called almost right away, "I'm not seeing anything. I'd just feel better if you would do this one right away."

As frustrating as the language barrier could be, there were also times when it was very useful. I felt completely comfortable with saying, "I'm not seeing anything," loudly across the hospital floor to Joanna, only because I knew that no one but Joanna and Steve would understand.

While I finished hanging the IV bag, Steve held the light and Joanna plunged her needle into the woman's arm. For a long while there was nothing as Joanna pricked and rearranged, searching.

Then . . .

"You're in!" Steve said. Even though Steve was not an official part of the medical team, he had been an active member long enough to know the procedure. Besides assisting with basic tasks on busy days, he had been in the thick of the tension several times. Before we got the IO drill, he had helped with the attempt to screw the needles in by hand. He had helped give feedings through NG tubes.

He handed Joanna the line, and the IV was good.

The young woman in Bed 4 had a constant stream of visitors.

There was one tall young man I noticed especially. He wore a black Cancun T-shirt, a metal necklace, and a heavy metal watch. I assumed he was her husband. A man in a red-trimmed, khaki-colored shirt (once again, much too large for him) talked to the man with the metal jewelry.

"Can you tell how well-to-do someone is by what they wear?" I asked Joanna. "Like Bed 4's family . . ."

"Yeah . . ." Joanna nodded about Number 4. "There are ways of displaying wealth. It can even be a problem in the church, this pressure between groups."

"This sounds familiar," I said. Some things are the same no matter where you go.

She explained that educated people in Haiti often have a long nail on their little finger. "But sometimes people have it who aren't even all that educated," she added.

The jewelry man had a gentle touch with the young woman, lifting her head for a drink and adjusting her pillow behind her head. The family continued to ask questions about her progress.

I was not impressed with the woman herself. Her expression seemed angry and annoyed whenever we would come close to take her vital signs. Most people tried not to make things difficult when we came for blood pressures. Some, like the mummy man in Bed 16, even tried to be helpful. But this woman's arm was a dead weight. I couldn't blame her for not wanting to wake up five times a night to have her blood pressure taken, but she could at least be civil, I thought.

After a few days of this, we found out that the young lady was only fourteen. The man with the metal jewelry, carefully helping her drink and asking after her health, was her father, not her husband.

Being only fourteen years old is not an excuse for being unworkable. But we had all been fourteen once, and our sympathy for her was suddenly much greater. I made an effort to smile more, look her in the eye, and show that I cared.

Mary and Becky, both nurses and not just students, had arrived from Ohio to replace Ethan and Anna. They brought a fresh supply of balloons, as well as royal blue curling ribbon, and hung balloons by the beds of the small children.

We even gave balloons to the visitors sometimes to keep them occupied. One bright-eyed little visitor wore a shirt that said, "Daddy's Girl: Wanted in Every State," and had a smile as wide as a crescent moon. She grew bored as she waited for her sister to recover from a bad case of cholera, so we showered her with stickers and balloons.

Of course we had never given a balloon to Number 4, because we thought she was far too old. One day someone gave her a balloon that was not blown up. I saw that she was fiddling with it, looking bored. I blew up another one for her and hung it by the head of her bed, hoping she would not be embarrassed. She wrote on it with a Sharpie, and later I saw her tapping it back and forth.

Her family kept asking about her because she recovered slowly. She did not want to eat.

"What do you think of our daughter?" They worried that she had something more than cholera.

"With cholera, it can take a few days to recover," Bethanie and Joanna reassured them.

When her IV clotted off, we thought she was well enough to be off the IV and just drink instead. But she did not want to drink.

"Okay," Joanna finally told her, "are you going to drink, or do you want us to put another IV in you?"

She wanted the IV back!

Overall, I wondered if the people of La Source showed more loyalty to their sick friends and family than the people of the American Midwest. I was struck with culture shock every time I saw a cholera bed passing by my bedroom window or pulling into our "ambulance bay" at 4 a.m., accompanied by ten or twenty people. Where did they all come from? I was pretty sure I didn't have twenty friends who would be happy to get up in the middle of the night to carry me several hours over a mountain.

CHAPTER 16

NO *IFS*

Mercy calls you break your chains . . .

One day one of our observation patients, an elderly woman, came into the hospital and settled herself on one of the beds. This normally was not allowed. Observation patients were required to stay in the observation tent until the nurse decided that they should be admitted to the hospital.

"Ummm . . . what's going on with this lady?" I asked Joanna. She laughed.

"Well, she's one of the local midwives. It wouldn't be respectful to tell her to move," Joanna said. We let her stay, and she was soon admitted anyway.

"Are the midwives good at their job?" I asked Bethanie later.

"Yes, most of them are," she said. "And they're usually good about calling me if something is going wrong."

Once, a local midwife gave a newborn baby a spoonful of the mother's blood to drink. The mother, who had HIV, was very upset. In their next workshop for the area midwives, Bethanie and Joanna addressed this and instructed the ladies NEVER to give babies a drink of their mother's blood.

"All the other midwives said that they had never heard of it, and they were all asking the lady who did it where *she* had heard it," Bethanie said, remembering the clamorous seminar with a smile.

Although most babies are born at home, the nurses sometimes sent women to a hospital if the baby was turned wrong or if there was risk for a difficult birth.

Many of the ladies were anemic, needing iron pills from the nurses at the clinic. In the United States, women are expected to have an iron (hemoglobin) count of 12, although sometimes this dips to 10 or 11 during pregnancy. In La Source, many of the ladies would come with an iron count of 8. The nurses would give the ladies iron pills, and their count would usually come up in time for delivery, reducing the risk of complications.

One woman, seven months pregnant with twins, came to the clinic with an iron count of 4.7. Although this was quite low, it was not unheard of in La Source, and the nurses thought that with two months left, she might have time to raise her iron levels by taking pills.

However, a few days later the woman began to go into labor. The labor stopped, but the nurses sent her to a hospital, where she was given blood transfusions. When the twins were born a few days later, both were alive, but one died shortly after birth.

When the lab tested the woman's blood after delivery, her count was down to 2.7. They gave her more blood and the story ended well. The woman and the living twin were soon discharged.

Another time, Bethanie was awakened at 5:00 on a Thursday morning by insistent knocking on her door.

"Tata had her baby, but we don't know if he's all right. He's just lying there. Could you come check on him?"

Joanna and Bethanie had been discussing Tata and her pregnancy two days before, because according to their dates the baby should have been born already.

"Do you think we should send her out to town since she's so overdue?" Joanna had asked Bethanie.

"Let's wait for one more week," Bethanie replied. The family was poor, and it wasn't as if it were Tata's first pregnancy: this would be her sixth child.

On Wednesday, the day after the discussion, Bethanie visited Tata. She reminded her to call the midwife if she thinks she is getting close to the birth.

That was yesterday.

These things flashed through Bethanie's mind as she stared at the early morning caller.

"He's not crying?"

"No, they have been banging on a plate, but he won't cry."

"Is he breathing?"

"We're not sure."

When Bethanie arrived, she found a dead baby. He had died in the prolonged birth process.

"Banging on a plate?" I asked Bethanie.

She was not sure what it meant either.

In one sense, even though they grieved, the people were fatalistic: what will be, will be. They would not have thought of blaming Bethanie for the death. In one breath they would say that it was the will of God, but in the next moment they might suspect a curse.

Tata, the mother of the dead baby, told Bethanie that she knew the baby would die because of a dream. "I knew we would lose him. You know those people already caused my seven-year-old son to die years ago . . ."

Another mother who lost a four-month-old child felt the same way. "She had blood in her mouth after she died," she told Bethanie. "Doesn't that prove that they put a curse on her?"

"I think her diarrhea and dehydration could have caused her to have blood in her mouth too. I don't think it was something someone did to her."

"No, they put a curse on her."

It made Bethanie wish the people *would* blame her instead of suspecting their friends and neighbors of putting a curse on them.

Like any group of people, however, Haitians are not all alike in their thinking patterns.

One time a family from church was expecting a baby. As the due date approached, several people told the family that they had a dream about the woman having a difficult delivery.

If it had not been a Christian family, Bethanie felt sure that they would have gone to the witch doctor for his interpretation of the dreams, and paid for charms and ceremonies to save the life of the baby and mother. Instead, the church family banded together. The church sisters met at the woman's house for prayer meetings, even praying that the family could have a comforting dream from the Lord.

Not only did God send a peaceful dream to the father, but the baby was born soon after without complications.

As they were rejoicing in God's blessing, the woman realized that something was not quite right. Bethanie found that the placenta had not been completely delivered, a serious complication with the risk of bleeding to death.

After feeling God's protection so closely with the fast and safe delivery, this was a blow, especially since it meant she would have to go to the hospital. However, God spared the woman's life, proving Himself a second time to be the Protector and Healer of the family.

Sometimes, going to the hospital didn't help.

Bethanie was awakened early on a Sunday morning in summer because a young lady, several months pregnant, was having seizures. She found the woman actively convulsing, with a blood pressure of 220/140. She knew it was eclampsia, a dangerous condition, so they quickly started off on the three-hour drive to the hospital in Gonaives. The woman regained consciousness on the trip, but began convulsing again as the vehicle bounced in to Gonaives and arrived at the hospital.

The hospital nurses immediately put in an IV and began giving her medication according to their standard procedure. The woman came out of her seizure, but was still groggy from the experience.

As the nurses began injecting magnesium sulfate, Bethanie noticed a change in the young lady's eyes. Suddenly she sat up.

"Please stop. I feel like I'm suffocating," she said. Then she lay down, dead.

Apparently she had a reaction to the magnesium.

On the long journey home, the vehicle rang with wailing and mourning. The next morning Bethanie attended the burial before going to the clinic to see more patients.

Besides working with local hospitals, Bethanie and Joanna would send patients to other clinics that offered services they did not. One afternoon a woman arrived in labor. She knew she needed to go to another clinic that did deliveries, but she wanted someone to take her. Steve agreed to take her. Darren, a young man visiting the clinic to help out for a few weeks, went with him. Darren hoped to become a doctor.

The men dropped the lady off at the clinic. They noticed a roadside soccer game and stopped to watch it. When the game was finished, they decided to go back to the clinic and check on the lady. She was at the point of delivery.

Immediately after birth, the baby girl was breathing, but not crying. Her skin was a grayish color. As Darren and Steve watched, the nurse on duty massaged her back. She took the bulb syringe and squeezed it in and out without taking it out of the nose, as if she had never used one before. The baby stopped breathing and the nurse seemed helpless.

Darren stepped in. He suctioned the infant correctly, gave the baby a few breaths, and started CPR. He prayed. Would the tiny baby start breathing again? Sure enough, soon after the prayer she began to breathe on her own. The mother named her Wozmika. She brought the little girl to the clinic for check-ups later, and Bethanie saw that she was normal and healthy.

What an experience for Darren as he thought about entering med school! And what an experience for everyone, when they thought about God's plan for the helpless baby. What if Steve had not been willing to make the drive? What if Steve and Darren had gone straight home after dropping the woman off? What if the soccer game had lasted longer? What if it had been shorter?

In *The Hiding Place,* Corrie ten Boom goes to the kitchen in the middle of the night because she hears her sister making tea. German and English planes are fighting above the city and she cannot sleep. There is an explosion, and when she returns to her room, she cuts her hand on a long, sharp piece of metal she finds on her pillow. As her sister Betsie bandages her cut hand, Corrie begins to say, "What if I hadn't heard you . . . ?" but Betsie stops her.

"There are no *if*s in God's world," she says.

With Wozmika too, there were no *if*s. God had brought a young man all the way from America to save her life.

And, if there were no *if*s for her, there were none for the lady with the twins either, or Tata, or the church family with the dreams, or the lady with eclampsia. Bethanie recognized this and tried not to blame herself, even if someone died. It was a temptation, but she realized that God was the one in charge.

For some mysterious reason God still chooses to use us as His instruments—earthen vessels that we are—with our limited knowledge, our narrow perspectives, and our bent toward error, mistakes, and sin, Bethanie wrote. *May it be that my mistakes . . . somehow help to demonstrate to the people here that my knowledge and skills are nothing without the excellency of the power of God.*

CHAPTER 17

PROBLEMS

His power increasing still shall spread . . .

We saw the house of one of La Source's five witch doctors when Bethanie took us on a tour of the area. It was marked with two flags on top of a pole. Bethanie told us that witch doctors usually have flags at their houses.

Joanna's brother, Bobby, had lived in La Source for a number of years. One evening as he headed home on the dusty white path that leads up to the mission houses, he felt an urge to stop at the witch doctor's house. With the sun dropping low in the sky, he found a seat on a log bench in the "waiting room," the stick-frame porch outside the witch doctor's workshop.

Kanès was a tall, bony man. Belonging to the same community, he and Bobby knew each other well. When he arrived, he sat down on the log bench beside Bobby.

"I came for a consultation," Bobby said, joking. Of course, the witch doctor knew that he was a Christian missionary.

"Come in," Kanès said.

Bobby followed him in, unsure what the invitation meant. As Kanès assembled images on his workbench and began speaking over them, all doubt left Bobby's mind. The witch doctor was, in fact, giving him a consultation.

A volley began between Bobby and the witch doctor, like a spiritual tennis game.

Bobby stood and began to pray in the name of Jesus.

Kanès began to drum, calling on the names of his gods, which were represented by more images on the floor of the workshop.

Bobby said, "In the name of Jesus, you can't bring up these spirits."

Kanès spoke louder.

Bobby continued to ask God to block the power of the witch doctor.

Kanès pranced back and forth, calling for the spirits louder and yet louder. Like the prophets of Baal leaping around the altar, he was desperate.

Bobby kept praying.

Kanès lurched toward Bobby.

Bobby stepped aside.

Kanès jumped back and forth, swinging his arms, pushing Bobby against the wall.

"I wasn't that afraid," Bobby remembers. "But I knew there was a possibility that the man was becoming dangerous."

A small crowd had gathered, some of them laughing. The witch doctor's half brother entered the workshop and urged Bobby to leave.

Bobby headed out, but Kanès came after him, hissing with rage.

"Get back!" he snarled at the crowd. "Don't you know I have power to send fire out of my mouth to burn you? Get back!"

The crowd moved back a little, but Kanès knew he had lost the contest. While Bobby continued to walk away, the witch doctor whirled back to his workshop.

He came back with a machete in his hand.

There was a gasp from the crowd as the witch doctor, machete in hand, followed Bobby. Would Kanès really resort to using a weapon just to prove a point?

"Jesus has the victory today!" Bobby called out. He was scared, but not paralyzed with fear.

"Jesus has the victory today!" he repeated.

Kanès pushed Bobby again, but not hard enough to throw him down. Then, waving the weapon, he made a half circle and went back into his workshop.

The show was over. The witch doctor had lost, with home field advantage.

"Are you okay?" the tense crowd asked Bobby. Some of them were laughing, but others were afraid.

Like Elijah on Mt. Carmel, Bobby pleaded with the crowd.

"Will you believe in the power of God above the power of the witch doctor? Will you come to deliverance in the name of Jesus?" He prayed with them before leaving for the night.

Why was I so naïve? Bobby remembers thinking as he continued up the path. *Why did I start in so lightheartedly?* Yet God had been able to use the situation for good. *I rejoiced that God had shown several people the truth of who is really God. How I longed for these people to find that liberating faith in Jesus Christ!* he wrote.

"Do the Christians go to the witch doctors?" I asked Bethanie.

There was no clear-cut answer to that. Certainly, many people who claimed to be Christians also went to the witch doctor with their problems. Bethanie said that it was a huge leap of faith for a person to truly abandon the witch doctor.

I could understand why the missionaries could get exhausted. The problems facing the Haitian church were different from the problems facing churches in the States. The pressure to subscribe to the witch doctor was one problem, but there were others. One that may seem small, but often caused frustration, was the lenient approach to time.

With our 24-hour scheduling at the hospital, I was able to attend church only once. I followed Joanna, who helpfully translated for me different times throughout the service.

The service started with singing at 9:30 and then moved to Sunday school. The problem was, very few were there at the beginning. Only the missionary families were present when the Creole singing began. When it was time for Sunday school, not enough children were present to have a class, so the little people stayed with the adult class.

The interesting thing was that the people *did* come—just not on time. By the time I slipped away for my shift, about halfway through the service, the front benches were packed with little boys and girls. Adults of all ages had filled the seats in the back. It had gone from looking like a dead church at the beginning of the service to appearing vibrant and thriving halfway through.

Although I could not understand Pastor Matt's remarks, I found out later what he said to the people after Sunday school.

"You like to discuss, and that's good," he encouraged. "But if we all come on time, there will be more time to discuss. Not even enough children were here for Sunday school!" Matt balanced his firm admonition with a personable, caring approach that gained him respect even as a newcomer to that part of Haiti. People could tell that he and his wife Sarah and their family considered Haiti to be their home. They had lived in Haiti almost from the time of their marriage.

At a tea party hosted by Matt and Sarah's daughter Esther, we learned more about the family's history. With her mother's help, seven-year-old Esther had spread out the tea party on the family's second-story porch. The open porch gave us overwhelming views of the mountains and valleys in the backyard. She set the glass tumblers for our iced tea on top of our paper plates to keep them from blowing away in the ever-present January breeze.

As we all nibbled on a delightful mixture of dried fruit and butterscotch chips, Esther told of their vehicle getting stuck in the mud on a family trip. They had gotten out and started walking, but soon someone came with a donkey for Sarah and the children.

"I can't remember if it was one or two donkeys," Sarah said, smiling as she remembered the shaggy adventure.

Sarah recalled the January 2010 earthquake, when they had lived in a different part of Haiti. Although they were not in Port-au-Prince near the epicenter of the earthquake, they saw much damage. They had no way of knowing the extent of the damage at that time, because their cell phone had quit working. But the fact that the cell phone tower had come down was a significant clue itself.

"My jar with the caterpillar fell down and broke, and the caterpillar got away," Esther remembered sadly.

Sarah, like Steve's wife Deborah, had given birth in Haitian hospitals. I could tell that there were very few pieces of Haitian culture that they had not accepted as their own, and I knew that this alone spoke volumes to the church people of La Source.

CHAPTER 18

ENTITLEMENT

Justice shall guard His throne above, and peace abound below.

Another significant problem was the idea of entitlement: people felt that they deserved to continue getting gifts if they received them once.

Internally I often react pretty strongly when I feel like someone feels entitled to something from me—when they feel like I owe it to them to give them something, Bethanie wrote.

It happened a lot, at the homes of the missionaries, on their property, and at the clinic.

"We're hungry," the two little girls at Bethanie's door said.

Bethanie had several bananas, so she gave one to each of the girls. Before saying "*Mèsi,*" one of the girls had a question.

"When shall we come back for something again?"

Bethanie laughed.

"I gave you something today—just today. That doesn't mean I'll have something for you again."

Once, the mission staff had been trying to fix leaks in the water pipe running from the mission compound down to the clinic. The pipe was lying uncovered one morning when a crowd came rushing up to Steve's house.

"Mizè cut the pipe! Water is gushing out!"

When the missionaries first moved to La Source fifteen years before, Mizè's family had sold them land on which to build their buildings. Mizè and his brothers felt that this sale should entitle them to full-time jobs from the mission staff. This had not happened and Mizè became angry.

Steve hurriedly turned off the water flow from the well and rushed down to see what was going on. Sure enough, the water was gushing from a gash in the pipe on which Mizè had taken out his bitterness. As Steve began to repair the pipe, Mizè intentionally stood in the way, trying to prevent the repair job.

Even at the clinic, where medicine was provided for a fraction of the true cost, some patients felt they were treated unfairly.

Although both HIV patients and tuberculosis patients were eligible for free food to help them stay healthy, there was a waiting list for this service. The clinic was able to give rice, beans, oil, and milk powder to 140 people, but there were 187 HIV and TB patients.

The newest patients went on the waiting list.

The problem arose with an HIV patient who had been coming to the clinic for four or five years, but had recently moved to another town. Bethanie wrote her a letter of transfer to the new hospital where she could receive care.

After a six-month absence, the woman returned unexpectedly to the clinic. Of course, by this time someone else had taken her place on the nutrition program.

Bethanie was very glad to see her. However, she was careful to explain that if the woman wanted to receive food again, she would have to go back on the waiting list. The woman took the news with surprising calm.

Bethanie moved on to another patient, but soon she heard a racket starting out in the hall.

"I paid a cycle to bring me here! What do you mean you're not going to give me food! How dare you!"

Not only was the woman shouting, but the employee in charge of handing out the food had raised his voice and was shouting back. Bethanie had never heard him raise his voice before in the five years they had worked together. She quickly left her patient and went out to investigate.

"I already explained to you that we don't have enough food for everyone to receive it right now," Bethanie said. "Your husband still receives it because he's been coming for his appointments faithfully. We'll give him oil, but he needs to have a container for us to pour it into."

"Humph. Well, I am not going to eat my rice dry. Give me the oil."

Of course, a crowd gathered, providing a running commentary of the debate.

"Listen to how she's talking to the nurse! Some people have no manners!"

"Try to borrow a container from someone in the area. Then we'll give your husband the oil," Bethanie repeated.

"Now you made me get angry. And because of this surge of blood it will be dangerous for me to cross the ravine, so I'm going to have to sleep here for the night. All because of you! And to think that I paid a cycle to come!"

Bethanie did not bother arguing with the local belief about the surge of blood and the ravine. She reminded the woman about her transfer to the other hospital.

"You wouldn't have had to pay a cycle to come over here," she added. "You could have just continued on at the other hospital. It was your choice to come. We didn't make you come."

Having stated the case kindly and clearly, Bethanie closed the door and returned to her other patient.

Remarkably, the same afternoon at the clinic, a little boy came up to Bethanie.

"The teacher sent me to you for school books."

"School books? I don't have any school books."

"*Wi*, school books."

He was a likable little fellow whose parents had both died of AIDS. Bethanie smiled at him, racking her brain for what he might be meaning.

"Did you bring some over for us to tape up for you?"

"No."

"Your teacher sent you here for school books?"

"*Wi*. He sent me to you for school books."

With a flash of memory, Bethanie recalled that she had given the boy money for his books the previous year. She remembered being disappointed later when he threw rocks at one of the mission vehicles when it did not stop to give him a ride somewhere. Bethanie explained to the boy that she had not promised to buy him books this year, and that she did not have the money for that.

Bethanie continued her thoughts about these encounters.

I've been struck with some irony in the situation. Why is it that I resent a sense of entitlement in other people? Isn't it because I myself feel entitled to certain things from them—things like gratitude, respect, appreciation? I have no more right to expect that of them than they do to expect other things of me.

CHAPTER 19

GAME TIME

And heaven and nature sing . . .

I was borrowing Bethanie and Joanna's computer to read e-mails from home when I came across this line from a friend: *Do me one favor. Ask one of the natives if they know what snowboarding is.*

Not having the Creole vocabulary to ask someone, I mentioned it to Bethanie and Joanna. They both laughed.

"It's hard enough to have a conversation about snow!" Bethanie said. She was certain that there was no Creole word for *snowboarding.*

All sports in Haiti were an afterthought to soccer. Even the basketball hoops in Port-au-Prince were afterthoughts, pinned into a tiny plot on the edge of a giant soccer field.

"The villages here all make up teams during the soccer season," Steve said, "but it's not organized to the point of training hard for it."

Soccer teams from La Source and surrounding areas had met in a grassy area for years to face off during the season. Now, walls of cement block were rising around the grass. According to rumor, an organization called CARE had donated $16,000 U.S. and approved its use for the "stadium." It could be seen from a distance, a symmetrical, box-like imprint on the wildly skewed and raw landscape. Though it may have been intended as a monument to wealth and progress, to many it seemed to be a memorial to careless money management. How many people could be fed with $16,000 U.S.?

A couple of times Ethan, Anna, and I saw a group of young boys playing soccer in an open area not far from the path leading from the mission compound to the hospital. I wondered if there were world-class soccer players here that had been missed by recruiters scouring the cities of the world.

Although I was not able to introduce snowboarding to the Haitians, I do believe that Mary and I get the credit for starting a new spectator sport in La Source: donkey riding. After Ethan had planted the idea in my mind when he casually mentioned that he would like to ride a donkey, my desire sprouted and grew. I continued to mention the idea until Bethanie made connections with Dyelès, a church member at La Source, and a ride was arranged for Mary and me.

Dyelès also works at the clinic and hospital. He and his wife are hospitable people who enjoy serving supper to the missionary staff on occasion. Dyelès and Mary had hit it off in the clinic one day when they attempted to have a conversation. Mary, with her spontaneous interest in everyone, was trying to learn some Creole and make friends.

That's when Dyelès said, *"Ve bisht du?"* (How are you?) His unexpected attempt at speaking Pennsylvania Dutch brought much amusement. From that point on their conversations were a disastrously funny melting pot of Pennsylvania Dutch, English, and Creole.

"What's the chance that we will get to have this donkey

ride *privately?*" I asked Mary as we followed Dyelès in the afternoon sunlight.

We looked at each other warily, realizing at about the same time that if we wanted to ride a donkey, we would probably be riding in front of the entire La Source community.

Dyelès led us to the side of the clinic where two donkeys stood placidly under a tree, unaware of the role they were about to play in the afternoon's festivities.

"Two donkeys?" Mary asked Dyelès, holding up two fingers.

"One donkey, one donkey," Dyelès said, holding up just one finger. "*Bourik,*" he added, teaching us the Creole word for donkey.

Apparently the other donkey was just tied there and was not actually ours to ride.

"You go first, and we'll take pictures of each other," I said. Unlike me, Mary had a few pages of donkey-riding history in her life story, and I was depending on her to set an expert example.

The donkey was pretty small, and Mary is tall, but she still struggled a little to mount the beast and settle on the wooden saddle.

"Is this right?" she asked Dyelès.

Apparently that was not in his list of English phrases, because he was not offering much help. Finally somewhat satisfied, Mary signaled that she was ready to go.

The donkey trotted across the side of the marketplace in La Source, with me snapping pictures on both of our cameras. At this point a crowd began to gather. Seeing the white woman on the donkey, the locals dropped what they were doing and ran after us. Dyelès pranced around the whole procession, laughing and probably poking fun at us in Creole.

Someone must have gone campaigning for a donkey for the other white woman who was walking. We had not gone far at all when more figures appeared on the path behind us, with a second donkey in tow. As the procession halted and the new donkey arrived to help with the fun, my anxiety level spiked.

We had asked Bethanie how they get on the donkeys.

"Oh, they take them against a bank or somewhere so you can stand on something a little higher," she said confidently, calming our fears.

They do not.

Yes, Mary had managed to struggle to the top of hers, but there were several points to consider. First, she is much taller than I. Second, the donkey they brought for me made Mary's donkey look like a beginner's toy. Mine was massive.

I decided firmly that I was not going to make a fool of myself by trying to mount the donkey and ending up with my nose in the rocks. I took off my flip flops and stuck them in the woven saddle bags. I don't know why, but that made me feel as though I was taking control of the situation.

"Tell him to put his hands together to form a step," Mary suggested helpfully from the top of her miniature donkey. The donkey's owner was a tall man of about fifty or sixty years. He was dressed in a white button-down shirt—several sizes too large, of course—orange plaid sweat pants, and a bill cap.

I wished I could tell him. The crowd, which was growing by the minute, stood watching me.

"It's too tall," I said in English, making height-expressive motions with my hands.

The tall man answered me in Creole, probably with some encouraging falsehood about how easy it is to get on a donkey.

"Too tall," I repeated with the same motions, determined to stand my ground.

For a second we all stood there helplessly. Then, without asking permission (or maybe he did in Creole), the donkey's owner picked me up in his arms and set me on the donkey.

As the sky lurched before my eyes, the noise of the crowd rose to a deafening shriek of laughter and shouting, as if someone had turned the volume dial. Mary, across the way on her donkey, shuddered with laughter and snapped photos.

"Oh, if only I would have gotten a picture of that!" she wailed, still shaking.

I took a sidelong glance at the tall, bony man, thinking, *I'm afraid I weigh more than you do. How in the world?* Sure that everyone else was thinking the same thing, I was glad for once that I could *not* understand Creole. Anyway, it took care of getting on the donkey, and we were ready for the ride.

The crowd marched us down the path with triumph, shouting and cheering with every step. People beside the road (who could hear us coming way out ahead) dropped everything and stared. Their expressions usually started with a blank stare as they saw the two white women appearing above a rise in the road. Some of their faces even had a trace of alarm. But by the time we were passing them, their faces split open with uncontrolled mirth.

One ancient woman saw us coming and stood frozen in horror inches from the path. I did not know if she was mad or scared, so I waved cheerily at her. At that, she burst into long gales of laughter, so loud that it outshouted the noise of our cheerful caravan. Clearly, this was the funniest thing she had seen in years, maybe decades. I don't know if she's still laughing or not, but I wouldn't be surprised.

We ended the ride by parading back through the main marketplace of La Source. Our entourage had saved its loudest, most expressive clamor for this moment. We passed the hospital. Over beside the clinic, Joanna was bending over a man on a stretcher, putting an IV in. A crowd of people surrounded her, and they all looked our way.

"It looked like the procession going into Jerusalem," Joanna said later.

Becky, our faithful friend who was working the shift while we provided the community with entertainment, said she heard the racket and thought it was a fight.

"All the visitors in the hospital looked at each other with questions in their eyes," she said, "and one by one they got up and went out to watch the show."

Joanna told us later that she suspects we may have started a new community activity.

"I think the people *really* enjoyed that," she told us.

"I suppose we made headlines in the La Source community newspaper," I said facetiously.

If they do turn donkey rides into the latest spectator sport of La Source, I hope they find a nice step stool somewhere. Unsuspecting Americans who may want to try the sport do not come pre-trained.

CHAPTER 20

FEARS

Faithful and pure, thy rays beam to save . . .

Protected by quarts of Clorox water and hand sanitizer, we did not worry too much about getting sick. Still, there was the splashing on our feet if someone missed the bucket, or the occasional rain of vomit on an unsuspecting taker of vital signs. We did talk a little about what we would do if we got cholera. Would we admit ourselves into our twenty-bed hospital with the holes in the beds? Top priority in everyone's mind was to drink lots of oral rehydration solution first, in an attempt to avoid the blue beds.

"Well, it will work out fine if I get cholera," Bethanie laughed. "I'll just give orders from my bed!"

Becky insisted that she would treat her cholera herself, in her own bed.

"What if you need an IV?" I asked.

"I'll have my IV in one hand, and I'll change the bags with the other," she said.

Of course, we knew that if one of the staff actually did contract cholera, we would have all banded together to care for our comrade with tireless devotion. But we warded off the thought of the dreadful possibility by joking about it.

There were more things than cholera to worry about. With IV fluids, cholera was a quick fix, usually. But when Joanna and Bethanie discussed the possibility that a patient had tuberculosis, I got nervous. If a patient had TB in the hospitals at home, he was put in isolation in a negative-airflow room and was required to wear a special mask in the hallways. Here it was treated in a much more casual manner.

I asked Joanna about tuberculosis one day.

"Yes, it is contagious," she agreed. The tuberculosis patients being treated at the clinic could easily spread the disease to others. With one cough, microscopic droplets become airborne and can infect the people who inhale them. Treatment for tuberculosis takes eight months. The clinic provides extra nutrition for the patients to help them recover more quickly.

In all her years of working with tuberculosis, Joanna had never tested positive for the disease. Of course, tuberculosis targets the weak and the sick. People with HIV are prime candidates for tuberculosis. But others can get it too. A twenty-year-old woman, having been the primary caretaker for her father who died of tuberculosis, tested positive for the disease. But with the clinic's new ability to test family members, patients could now be treated before they got sick.

"I just have to give all the honor to God for being protected," Joanna said, shaking her head in amazement. "I have never had a problem with it all these years."

Joanna constantly glorified God's blessing in the good things of life.

Besides HIV patients in the cholera hospital, caring for people with the disease was a major week-by-week task at the regular clinic. About 160 HIV or AIDS patients came to the clinic on Mondays and Thursdays. Some of these were children, like the baby with cholera, who had gotten the disease from their mothers.

Of course, there is no cure yet for HIV or AIDS. With medications, however, years can be added to the lives of the victims. Even just a few extra years make a big difference to a mom with little children. Also, by giving medications to babies born to HIV-positive moms, the nurses have been instrumental in keeping some of the babies from getting HIV. The mom drinks the medicine during delivery of the baby, and the baby is given medicine within seventy-two hours of birth. Instead of breastfeeding, the mom feeds the baby with a bottle.

Bethanie told us that in Africa the risk of disease from waterborne illness is so high that HIV moms are told to breastfeed their babies anyway. There, the risk of getting a disease from the bottle is greater than the risk of getting HIV from the mother. But here in La Source (other than during the time of the cholera epidemic, perhaps), water was not so dangerous.

Without medicine, many moms with HIV will pass the disease on to their babies. In fact, before the clinic started the medicine program for HIV babies, 56 percent of these babies died before they were eighteen months old, and others who lived tested positive for the disease. Only 19 percent did not have the disease.

After they started giving the medicine and having the babies drink formula, only 6 percent of the babies died before eighteen months, and 87 percent did not have the disease at all. *Talk about a fulfilling job!* Bethanie wrote at the end of a description of the clinic's HIV program.

Of course, HIV is not a disease like tuberculosis that travels through the air, but it is possible to get it from an infected person's blood. If a nurse accidentally pokes herself with a needle from an HIV patient, it would be possible for her to come down with the disease.

My scraped knee bothered me. Before coming to Haiti, I had debated getting a tetanus shot, knowing that I was due for one, but I had not gotten it done. Now I had fallen and cut myself in a pasture, just the kind of place where people get tetanus.

Anna had told me to put antimicrobial cream on it, but I had been too lazy to do so. Looking through *Merck's Manual,* which had useful information about tetanus, I read that one way to keep tetanus from developing was to disinfect the area.

"I should have listened to you, Anna," I said.

"I'll give you a tetanus shot if you want one," Bethanie said. She agreed to give me one after lunch the next day.

Lunch was made each day by a Haitian lady and served in an open shed to the missionary families. The food was also sent down to the people working at the clinic and hospital. It was packaged in a marvelous tin stacking device that made me wonder why we did not have such things in the United States. It looked like three tin buckets stacked on top of each other, with the bottom of one forming the lid of the next. The buckets had something like belt loops on them, and a slender metal piece belted them together on both sides so there was no danger of the stack toppling apart. Usually the bottom two buckets were filled with rice, and the top one held an oily red sauce with onions. In another container off to the side, there was often a meat of some kind: chicken wings, baked to a crisp, or a dry kind of meatballs that I came to appreciate.

Some of the visiting staff reported getting sick on the food, but I ate it almost every lunch and never felt any side effects.

We ate our lunch in the clinic office, a white room trimmed in the bright blue-green that must have been over-manufactured in Haiti's paint factories, judging by its common appearance. The room looked busy with filing cabinets, a refrigerator for vaccines, an autoclave on a gas burner, and a topographical map of Haiti spread on the desk. The forms and notes, lying on the desk or posted on the wall, were almost all written in Creole.

When I finished my lunch, Bethanie came and began poking around in the vaccine fridge, and I braced myself for the shot. I knew they were painful shots. In fact, people usually complained about having a sore arm for several days. But I was determined, and I knew the peace of mind would be worth it.

"Oh, I forgot. We're out of that one," she said matter-of-factly. "I would give it to you if I had it." Smile.

Now I was scared again. I knew the chance was ridiculously low, but what if . . . ? Tetanus was curable, but only if you got immediate medical treatment. Even Port-au-Prince, the capital, did not have cutting-edge medical care, and that was seven hours away.

"Actually, in Europe they don't even give booster shots," Bethanie said. "Only in the United States and Canada."

This was reassuring. Surely the risk was very low indeed. But there must be some reason the United States and Canada still recommended them, right?

I knew that Bethanie herself took risks in her attempt to save lives. One morning a cholera bed arrived with a dying man.

Anna saw him grimace once, and then he lay still. Thinking that maybe they could revive him with fluids, Bethanie instructed Anna to do chest compressions. She herself gave the man a few rescue breaths.

"There was vomit on his mouth," she said later. "He wasn't vomiting right then; it had been earlier, so it was dried, but it still made me nervous." Body fluids from cholera victims are highly contagious.

The man, who was dead on arrival, did not revive. Bethanie gave the friends and family the normal instructions about wrapping the body in the gray tarp and putting Clorox-soaked cotton in all body cavities.

"I feel bad," Joanna told me one time. "Most of our deaths have been on Bethanie's shifts. That's a lot of stress to deal with, and I've been getting off easy."

I was impressed with her compassionate attitude. Unlike many co-worker relationships, Bethanie and Joanna were quick to talk about each other's good qualities. In an end-of-year review, Bethanie wrote, *Joanna . . . has been one of the primary persons responsible for helping to make this year an enjoyable one for me. She's the kind of nurse you'd want to take care of you or your loved ones if faced with an illness.*

The men took the body away. Steve later heard that they took the body high up on the mountainside, where they dug a generous hole. They mixed two bags of cement, an expensive purchase. After placing the body in the bottom of the hole, they dumped the cement in on top.

Neither Steve nor Bethanie were quite sure why they did this. Apparently they wanted to be safe, a little like the nursing student from Indiana begging for a tetanus shot.

. . . .

"I have a cramp in my leg," Anna said to me one night when we actually met in our closet-like bedroom. For the most part, one of us was either working or sleeping. "You know that's a symptom of cholera, right?"

After night shift one time, I mentioned to Anna, "I went to the bathroom twice tonight. Do you think that's a sign of cholera?"

When she laughed at the fear, I went on. "Or tuberculosis, or tetanus, or HIV?"

Laughter, the best medicine.

Ethan dreamed one night that he was counting drip rates and could not get it to come out right no matter how he adjusted the roller clamp. I dreamed of a cholera bed, drawn by a team of horses, coming down the snow-covered avenue where I had grown up in Wisconsin.

But if we, with two weeks' experience, were dreaming of drip rates and cholera beds, what were Bethanie and Joanna dreaming?

"God has been so good," they said.

With the flurry of activity, the dozens of patients, the unco-operative drip rates, the brutal wind whipping the tarp walls, and the hot sun scorching us, I knew that must be it.

Joanna and Bethanie constantly mentioned all the ways that God had blessed them during the cholera epidemic. They were grateful for the volunteers. They were amazed that the hospital was exactly the right size. If it had been any smaller, it would have been too small for the busiest days. God had also provided the exact number of beds needed. Several times every bed and mat had been in use, but there had always been enough beds.

I had worked with busy nurses elsewhere and seen their

frustration and anger with half a dozen patients or a student nurse like myself. Here in La Source, in the midst of desolate mountains, in the epicenter of vomiting, sickness, and death, the head nurses, working 24/7 between the two of them, were smiling at the end of every sentence. We knew that God's goodness and grace were enabling them to maintain a peaceful attitude.

CHAPTER 21

NIGHT SHIFT

Guiding the pilgrim through the night . . .

Night shift in the blue glow was not predictable, other than that you would be besieged by crickets. These were not the benign crickets of my childhood. They were awful, fat, blackish brown dive bombers that attacked with a cracking noise and clung to their victims. The buzzing, humming sound they made was interrupted by a metallic cracking as they collided against things or people.

In addition to these normal hazards of the night shift, a neighbor close to the hospital was making charcoal. By the time I arrived at 9:00 for the night shift, a heavy charcoal odor had seeped into the hospital and a haze frosted the blueness.

Mary was coughing and sneezing by the time she left, saying that she was glad she was not working the night shift. "Thanks, Mary," I said wryly. By this time, however, after having experienced celebrity status together on the donkey ride, we were good friends.

As if the assault on our lungs was not enough, another neighbor was hosting a voodoo party with music cranked to a high volume and drumbeats throbbing in the air. The noise went on late into the night, and people passed back and forth in front of the hospital, their footsteps crunching on the white stones.

The voodoo, the curses, and the witch doctors held a frightening fascination to naïve North Americans like me. Bethanie told of a thirty-year-old man who was studying to be a witch doctor when he fell ill. He concluded that another witch doctor was jealous of him and sent the illness as a curse. Ironically, he turned to the witch doctors for help, visiting workshop after workshop for consultations. After seeing twenty-one witch doctors in an effort to get the curse removed, he came to the clinic. Bethanie and Joanna easily diagnosed him with tuberculosis. Although the disease can be fatal if not treated, it is completely curable.

Seizing the chance, the nurses gave the man a New Testament and talked to him about his spiritual future.

In the nurses' daily work at the clinic, they often got the chance to talk to people who normally would not listen to a Christian. With their loose morals and multiple wives, many of the witch doctors had HIV. They received medication for both their bodies and their souls.

Another time, Joanna spoke to a woman with terminal cancer. Joanna broached the topic of life after death, and the woman showed interest in what she had to say. Although Joanna could not know for sure what effect the conversation had, the woman began attending church in her home area and showing interest in spiritual things.

Tonight we felt that, like the man with tuberculosis, our physical and spiritual health was being attacked with the charcoal and the voodoo. At least the wind was still, which meant the tarp was not flapping loudly. And the roosters were lying low for the time being.

The permanent clinic building, across the dusty white path, became a bit of an oasis to us, especially at night. We would slip over to the gas stove and heat water, sometimes to heat IV bags for a patient receiving a lot of fluids, and sometimes to make ourselves a nice English toffee cappuccino.

I felt a little fear when slipping across the dark, empty lot and into the empty building with only the aid of my flashlight, but not as much as I would have felt in the United States under the same circumstances. An air of safety surrounded us. Bethanie said the people respected the clinic and hospital enough that she would not expect them to cause problems.

Even the lonely trails winding through the bushes felt safe. When I turned around on the path one time and saw a man with a machete behind me, it scared me a little. But then I realized that, of course, he was just going to chop down a sapling or do some other practical task.

I learned to laugh with the small, haggling boys saying, "Give me *dola*" (dollar). I assumed they were passing the time by annoying me, and not necessarily planning to steal or pillage. I talked to them in English, and they talked to me in Creole, and we laughed.

As I made my first round for nighttime vital signs, I was reminded why I disliked the nighttime vital signs routine. I especially disliked taking blood pressures on the patients with their IV arm close to the aisle. This meant that I had to reach across them to take their blood pressure in the other arm.

Just that morning I had thought of a clever idea to help solve the problem of the inside arm blood pressures. Joanna had admitted a fifty-year-old observation patient when she could not find a blood pressure on him anymore. His name was Derilès, and the nurses knew him and his family well because they had taken care of a family member desperately ill with tuberculosis. We had a child in need of an IV at the same time, so I was assigned to start Derilès' IV.

I will solve this problem of having to reach over people, I told myself. *I'll just climb up on the bed and use his inside arm for the IV, instead of the outside arm.* I knew that a little bit of inconvenience now would spare me a lot of trouble that night when I had to take five blood pressures on this man.

Derilès was groaning, tossing, guarding his abdomen, and sweating profusely. He had veins that looked wonderful, although when I rubbed his arm with alcohol, they seemed to invert, as if they were completely empty and the outside wall of the vein was taking on the shape of the inside wall. I tried one and got a flash, but that was it. Before I could try again, he turned his whole body away from me and began to vomit into the bucket at the side of the bed. The typical cholera vomit, something close to pure water, gushed from his mouth.

I finally got a 20-gauge catheter into a large vein along the inside of the elbow. I was quite pleased that I had remembered to choose the right arm. Now, for the rest of his stay, I would get to take his vital signs on the aisle side of the bed.

I went off duty and returned later for the night shift.

The day had been a scorcher. It had been so hot, in fact, that the gentleman with the wonderful veins had moved his pillow from the head of his bed to the foot of his bed to get away from the sun beating in through the blue tarp. He had done a complete flip, and his IV arm was now on the aisle side. For the rest of his stay, I leaned over him to take his blood pressure on the inside arm, straining my back like I had done so many times before. At least Derilès was a nice man who seemed to appreciate the care we were giving him.

Between the charcoal smoke, the "inside vital signs" arms, the supersized crickets, and the voodoo party, it was an exhausting night. Then I failed to get new IV fluid bags for both Bed 20 and Bed 18. Although I found them quickly, by the time I tried to flush them, both had clotted off to complete uselessness.

Number 20 was stable, and we decided to let him go without an IV and just watch him. Number 18, however, a young girl who could barely stand having tape removed from her skin, had to have an IV. We would have to stick her again.

She missed the bucket, creating a puddle on the floor, so we waited while her mom mopped it up. Crouched on my knees on her blue Hawaiian print sheet, I felt over and over again for veins, but I missed both times I tried. Joanna, however, was able to nail a vein on the first try. She was giving Bethanie a break from the night shift. After assisting me with the IV, she settled down to get some rest.

Joanna also had the gift of remembering who to think about when she woke up in the middle of the night. I was partway through taking vitals when I realized that Joanna had begun to stir. She was worried about Number 19, a little boy.

"He's just so restless, as though almost in shock." The little boy shared a sheet with his mother and had been lying awake. Joanna increased his IV rate and instructed me to put another 500 ml in fast.

The worst part of night shift was from about 2 a.m. to 5 a.m. As the night wore on with the charcoal smoke and the voodoo party still in the air, a desperate desire for sleep took over. I wanted to do whatever it would take to lie down for a nap.

We were allowed to sleep if things were quiet, and we had an alarm clock to get us back up for the next IV bag or set of vital signs. I stretched out the last foam mattress and fell into a deep sleep.

I was awakened after twenty minutes or so by a girl caretaker from Bed 10. She wanted more oral solution for the man to drink. Also, his IV site was leaking. I stumbled around in a haze for a few minutes. It was so cold!

I returned to my mat to wrap myself in my throw, but I knew I would not get any more sleep. The rafter-created triangle of sky at the open end of the hospital was a hazy gray. Every time I looked again, it was as if another squirt of white paint had been mixed into the gray and the triangular portion of sky had been repainted. Joanna got up and folded her sheets, taking her mat back to the clinic.

I learned two things that morning at the end of the long, choking night shift.

First, the Haitian people are devoted teeth brushers. That morning I noticed Number 4, Number 20, and Number 18 all brushing their teeth at the same time. This surprised me.

"Oh, that's very typical," Joanna told me. "If anything, the Haitian people might be more diligent at brushing their teeth than Americans."

Second, I learned that many Haitians, especially those who had worked at clinics in the past, tried to make a profit by reselling medication.

A man came up to Joanna and quietly asked her a question. Even though I did not understand the question or the answer,

I knew that Joanna had told him no.

"He wanted heartburn medication," she said, shaking her head. "I told him to go to another neighboring clinic. It's so hard with meds here. People are supposed to have a prescription with a stamp on it before they get them." She knew there was still corruption in the system.

Derilès, the man who changed positions, set the record for the greatest total fluid output in the cholera hospital. Over the course of his stay there, he lost 80 liters of fluid, or about 176 pounds, mostly vomiting and diarrhea.

Bethanie and Joanna had a special concern for Derilès. He was the father-in-law of a member of the church. He had taken care of a relative sick with tuberculosis. Although they had been taking this relative to the witch doctor, Derilès finally brought him to the clinic in a wheelbarrow. When the sick relative had recovered, one of Derilès's family members began attending church. But not Derilès. He was not interested in learning to know God.

As Derilès recovered in the cholera hospital, Bethanie tried to talk to him about his spiritual condition. Surely after his brush with death and his 80-liter fluid loss, he would think twice about his soul. But her words seemed to fall on deaf ears.

I'm hoping to pay him and his family a visit again in the near future, Bethanie wrote. She hoped that just as God used them to allow life to continue flowing in Derilès' physical body, He would enable them to influence the man to choose spiritual life as well.

CHAPTER 22

NUMBER 20

He comes to make His blessings known, far as the curse is found . . .

"These people have ways of killing other people silently through the witch doctor," Joanna said. We were sitting at the nurses' station, once again taking advantage of the language barrier to discuss Number 20, only a few yards away. "It just seems like he's been into something."

It had been a dangerous move. Number 20, a tall young man, had been at a different hospital, but he said he received poor care there. It had taken them two hours to transport the sick man by cycle to our facility. When he arrived, he had no measurable blood pressure and no radial pulse.

I inserted a 22-gauge catheter into a perfectly straight vein in his forearm. In half an hour his pressure was 144/40. At the next measurement, his systolic pressure was 176 with an almost bounding radial pulse.

Bethanie reported from the Creole conversations that the young man, probably in his twenties, thought he was going to die—that he had more than just cholera.

"They said this sickness is combined with something else," Joanna said. She knew they meant something spiritual, like a curse. "He's terrified."

The next morning the witch doctor came to visit.

Mary, my fellow donkey-riding volunteer, said he did not look like a witch doctor. And he didn't do anything scary; he just chatted. But the witch doctor's visit confirmed Bethanie and Joanna's suspicions that the young man feared something that could not be fought off with IV fluids.

Although they operated a dark business, even the witch doctors appreciated medical help. One time when Bethanie was treating an area witch doctor for his HIV, the man told her how much he appreciated one of the missionaries who had helped him in the past. The witch doctor said that he always speaks about that person with respect.

"You know, I think that person would prefer that, instead of only speaking well of him, you would choose to follow the same path in life that he is following," Bethanie told the man.

The witch doctor had replied, "Well, that's not impossible. I've thought about it before. Other people have encouraged me too, but . . . not yet."

Number 20's companions were an unsmiling bunch, dressed in black shirts that actually fit, unlike their many counterparts lost in baggy polos. These young men were not going to wear the castoffs of some tubby American.

They told Joanna that they did not like the other hospital because there they only treated him with IV fluids and oral rehydration solution.

"But that *is* the treatment for cholera!" Joanna told them.

I watched them closely as they listened to Joanna. They must have been brothers. Not only were they identical to the patient, they were identical to each other. They were both tall and lean and unsmiling. They stood at the head of their brother's bed, across from Joanna. Although the one had a cell phone in his hand from which he was texting, they both gave her full attention, their dark, unsmiling eyes focused on her gentle face. They picked up her every word, nodded almost in unison, and said little.

Apparently they wanted a hospital that would treat a curse too. Although they were clearly unhappy to be there, I wondered if they had been attracted by the missionaries' foundation of faith.

Did the young patient have reason to fear revenge?

He wrapped himself in a Lion King sheet and disappeared from the world. He did not quite have the skill of wrapping himself in a perfect mummy shape like Number 16 under his huge gingham checks. Most adults, in fact, stretched out comfortably when they slept. Not Number 20. He was often curled in a protective, almost fetal position.

Several times when I woke him to take his blood pressure, he would jump and pull away. When he would see that it was just someone there to take his blood pressure, he would relax and be workable, although not helpful.

He did not do much talking or smiling, and his blood pressure was always high.

Taking blood pressures on most people was a tricky maneuver of slipping the cuff around their arm and trying to get a fit in the available space. Not so for Number 20. His upper arm was so long that I had to decide on which part of it to place the cuff.

"He looks like such a basketball player!" I told Joanna. But there is no basketball in La Source.

That same morning one of the men came to the card table.

There was a string of Creole, which I did not understand, but I knew that Joanna had kindly told him no about something, punctuated with one of her trademark smiles.

"Number 20 wants to go out and sit in the sun," she translated to me when the brother walked away. "I told him I don't blame him for wanting to, but we've had too many problems with taking the IVs outside. They stop dripping, they clot off, and we have to put a new one in. It's just too much hassle."

"Would it be okay if I would go with him?" I asked. I had an odd sympathy for this terrified young man with the basketball player's arms and unsmiling face.

"Sure, if you want to take the time," she said.

When he unwrapped himself from the Lion King sheet, he was in fact wearing a basketball jersey with a number 11 on the back. I was astonished.

I took down the IV bag and the wire S-hook and followed a few feet behind Number 20. Already the drip rate had slowed, but that was because I could not hold it high enough above his head. As we went out toward the observation tent, I noticed the shiny pink handkerchief in his back jeans pocket. It was a charm, Bethanie told me, like many people wore to save themselves from curses.

He settled on the white, dusty ground on the outside corner of the observation tent, facing the marketplace. I found a place to hook the S-hook into the sapling joint of the tent.

I could not help asking.

"Do you play basketball?" I motioned to his shirt.

"*Wi,*" he said right away.

I knew he probably did not understand my English, but from the speed with which he recognized the word "basketball," I thought perhaps he truly did play.

"I think there might be a hoop in the area where he comes from," Joanna said. "There aren't any around here."

I stayed out in the sun not far from him, taking in the sights of the marketplace around me: a little boy with an upturned jug on the top of a stick, coconut cookie wrappers in the white stones by my feet, three donkeys and a cycle parked at the clinic, a woman with a huge basin on her head, and a man with a five-gallon jug on his shoulder.

A man in a short-sleeved orange dress shirt and Pennzoil bill cap came up to my patient. He said what must have been "hello" and did something I could not remember having seen before in the La Source marketplace—shook hands. It was the lightest, quickest of shakes, the brush of fingers, but it still seemed to come from somewhere other than La Source.

I kept checking his IV drip rate, sometimes adjusting the roller clamp slightly to keep it running at 30 drops per 15 seconds.

His brother brought him a lime soda from one of the vendors, the same kind I had gotten on our journey to La Source when we stopped for fried *bannann*. I frowned, and after checking with Joanna, vetoed the drink with English and gestures. "Bethanie says no sodas, no caffeine." I brought him the drink from beside his bed instead. The man who had brought him the soda helped him open the plastic tab at the top of the carton.

Even though his caretakers were silent and tense, they did know how to take care of him. The men helped him wash up and brush his teeth and stayed the night with him. I never saw any women there.

When it was time for me to take vital signs again, we went back in. He seemed exhausted and glad to curl back up on his bed.

When the rest of the story trickled in, we found out there was a reason no woman was present. Number 20's wife had died two weeks before in the same hospital he had just left. Number 20 did *not* think that his wife had cholera. She had severe abdominal pain, he said.

Even though abdominal pain *is* a symptom of cholera, it was easier to sympathize with him after we heard his story. No wonder he mistrusted the other hospital and suspected a curse. No wonder his own abdominal pain scared him. No wonder he curled up under the Lion King sheet, tried to hide from the world, and remained unsmiling.

Actually, I saw him smile once. I was ready to leave La Source for the first leg of our journey back to Port-au-Prince. He was sitting outside the hospital, in a change of clothes. The IV line was gone, so I knew he had been discharged. He saw me and smiled.

I wondered if the shiny pink charm had been transferred to his new back pocket and if he thought the handkerchief and the witch doctor's visit had healed him. I hoped that, like the witch doctor with HIV, Number 20 would remember us with respect. I hoped that he would embrace the grief of his wife's death and allow it to point him to an all-powerful God, and that he would trade in the shiny pink charm for a faith that did not depend on handkerchiefs. I hoped he would not make the mistake of saying "not yet."

CHAPTER 23

BREAD AND WATER

Richer by far is the heart's adoration; dearer to God
are the prayers of the poor . . .

Despite the problems in La Source, I will always think of it as a place of sunshine and beauty. Even the dark evenings at the end of December grew on me. As the wind howled and the windmill screamed and the trees danced, I wondered why La Source was not a tourist attraction. La Source owns a sense of enduring peace stamped in the dust of the white stone paths.

My trip to Costa Rica soon after my mom's death had been an experience of the grace of God. I knew already, without thinking things over, that my trip to La Source would remain in my mind as an experience of peace. My sister, who visited southern Haiti a few weeks after me, agreed.

That was one of the biggest things that made an impression on me: the healing of going to a place so raw and original, she wrote to me. *So few distractions, just the roar of people during the day who rise with the sun and go to bed with it, and the blackness of night with the full moon being the only lighting. And so many people who had so little.*

When I went to my shifts, down the green-lined paths that

twisted delightfully and confused strangers, I knew that other people would love this perfectly unspoiled world if they only knew about it. I did not wish for La Source to be overrun by Westerners; I just found that there are truly places left in the world that the guidebooks don't talk about. I knew why people didn't come; they thought it was dirty and poor. But the longer I lived in this "dirty and poor" corner of the world, the less certain I was that it was either truly dirty or truly poor. This belief grew on me the day we visited the bakery and the spring.

Bakery to me means the cupcake shop in Elkhart with its cheery lime-green tables and twelve daily flavors, or Panera Bread's fat oatmeal-sprinkled loaves, or Main Street Coffee's white chocolate raspberry scones. Over the Christmas season, *bakery* means red and green sprinkles and cinnamon rolls and peppermint and spice and gift boxes.

Bethanie took us to the stone bakery on a hot afternoon. It was dark inside, so the first thing we saw was the fire crackling deep inside a long, flat oven. A chicken sauntered in, picking at the dirt floor for stray bits of bread.

I wondered what the ten or so young people were doing here. Was the local bakery the community hang out? One of them was sleeping in the corner right inside the door, and I nearly stepped on her.

Off to the left, flat blankets of dough had been spread out to rise. They were covered with something that looked like wax paper. Twigs weighted the paper down so it would not blow away.

"The Haitian people do a better job than Americans do at covering food and drink," Bethanie told us. "As soon as they set food out for a meal, it gets covered unless you are eating right away."

To our right stood an imposing metal rolling machine, forbidding careless fingers to come near. Bethanie explained that the dough is fed through this machine. It is then cut into round shapes about the size of a bagel without the hole in the middle. Above our heads was a ten-foot-long wooden paddle suspended from the ceiling, used to position things in the blazing oven. A stack of battered metal baking sheets rose in the back of the bakery.

Bread was the only thing produced in the bakery. Vendors sold the bread, bagged up in silvery plastic bags with red or blue stripes, in the outdoor marketplace. I tasted this bread several times, and I loved it. It was chewy, almost like French bread. On New Year's Day I dunked it in the syrupy sweet coffee, as the local people do.

Sadly, we had not come at the right time to see the baking in action.

"They wait to bake until the fire burns down to just coals," Bethanie explained.

Everyone in the community could use the bakery. Most people did not have ovens, so they would bring their bread here, along with wood to fuel the fire.

As we continued on to the spring, I thought about my world as it was at holiday time. The little town of Nappanee with its brand-new supermarket, full of holiday baking supplies, giant glazed poppy seed muffins, poinsettias, popcorn tins, and expensive chocolates; the Amish Acres tourist attractions; the state-of-the-art library; the fall apple festival; coffee and pizza shops, and classy Christmas decorations. Haiti was missing all of these things.

We walked on to the spring. We took a turn on the path and suddenly saw palm trees! I also saw the orange flowers again, the lone splashes of color in a colorless land. Awed by the beauty of the oasis, we stopped to take pictures with the palm trees in the background.

Our footsteps took us down closer to the stream. Here, people washed both their clothes and themselves. Modesty was not a big concern, with children throwing off all their clothes shamelessly and adults showing little reserve themselves.

We stepped through the shallow creek, feeling the wonderful coolness of the water on our feet. Children played here. Maybe they were supposed to be bathing, but there was also a lot of splashing going on as they reveled in the freedom of the water.

The spring itself bubbled out of the ground, almost under the high cliff at the side of the creek. The water was cold and good, except after a heavy rain. Nelson had roofed the top of the spring area with a cement slab to keep debris from falling in from above.

A young boy crouched in the spring, filling jugs with water. He kept his feet behind the rock boundary so that the inner pool of water, bubbling out of the ground, would be kept clean. Other empty plastic jugs circled the spring.

This was not what I had pictured the "dirty and poor" country of Haiti to look like. What I had actually pictured, I could not remember. Trash, maybe. There was hardly any trash here. Screaming children, possibly. There were screaming children here in the coolness of the stream, but they were screaming with laughter as they splashed each other. What child isn't happy playing in a creek, without the pressure to get a tan or make the swim team?

As we crossed back over the creek, I realized that La Source is missing some things besides the glamour of civilized society. La Source is missing the faces of strain and stress. It is missing the young people at the festivals, trying to outdo each other with pricier clothes and more fantastic Christmas plans, driven to reach a standard set beyond their reach by places like Beverly Hills. The food thrown away after Christmas. The librarians, bored with the perfectly placed holiday décor. People at the coffee shops, hiding their stressed faces behind their computer screens and drinking away their loneliness with peppermint mochas.

We left the cool atmosphere around the spring and headed up the steep hill to the path. We struggled just to get to the top of the hill. The local women walked up the same path, balancing five-gallon buckets of water on their heads.

Perhaps it was no use comparing the problems in one country with the problems in another. No matter where a person lived, or whether he was worried about a curse or credit card debt, what mattered was that he knew where to go for help.

Jesus said, "I am the bread of life; he that cometh to me shall never hunger; and he that believeth on me shall never thirst" (John 6:35).

CHAPTER 24

IF AN EVACUATION BECOMES NECESSARY

The glories of His righteousness, and wonders of His love . . .

The Christmas season was over, and so was my time in La Source. Mary and I would make the trip back to Port-au-Prince, from where we would fly to Miami, and then on to our final destinations. The "Merry Christmas" blanket was packed back into my suitcase, which was tied to the top of the Land Cruiser.

Here in La Source, the blue hospital looked exactly as it had on Christmas Eve, only less busy. The cholera would not leave overnight, but it had peaked. There would likely be more and more empty beds until finally the blue cholera hospital could be turned into a marketplace again. The busiest week had been the one right before Christmas—a bit like America.

But there was no after-Christmas stress here. The economy was the same bustle of shoppers at the food stand, young people at the bakery, and moms getting water at the spring. The rugged mountainsides had not lost any decorations. No one was dealing with post-holiday stress syndrome or trying to kill themselves. No masses of shoppers were returning Christmas gifts they did not want. The little food stands outside the hospital were not packaging their Christmas décor in Rubbermaid totes for next year. No one was starting an exercise program or diet plans and wishing they hadn't spent so much money on Christmas or eaten so much food.

Mary and I sat in the second seat of the Land Cruiser. Matt and Steve were on top of the Land Cruiser arranging the luggage and strapping on a tarp because it was about to rain. In the cargo space behind the seats, about eight locals from La Source packed in, willing to endure the tight space for a ride to Gonaives.

"Do you have room for another person back there?" Steve asked Mary and me. It was not hard for us to make room for the young Haitian girl who crawled in beside us. More people had also crawled in the back. I was certain we were at maximum capacity.

Steve opened the driver's door, grabbed his laptop bag off the middle seat, and handed it back to us.

"One more coming up here," he said.

The airlines tell you, "If an evacuation becomes necessary, leave all personal belongings behind." Then the screen shows a photo of a man reaching for his laptop bag, and a bold, red X slides over the screen. The hint is obvious: When a plane goes down, it's not smart to worry about anything that does not have a living soul.

As Steve hauled over ruts, avoided rocks, and crossed the shallow water of the same riverbed four times, he reported that they had previously packed twenty-two people into the vehicle at one time. Granted, some of them had been children, but the point was that we were not, in fact, at maximum capacity.

As the roadway stretched on, he and Matt began to discuss, in English, some of the cultural issues that were affecting the church. The Haitians in the La Source church were slow to embrace the responsibilities of leadership. They did not want to be blamed for something the others did not like. There were disagreements about education, voting, finances, and the local school.

"It bothered me that no one said, 'Now what does Scripture say about this?' " Matt said, recalling a recent church discussion.

The Land Cruiser bounced on through the brown and green landscape and over a cement bridge with election graffiti painted on the one flat surface. We passed cactuses and small huts. At one point a donkey stood in our path. Steve slammed on the brakes, and the truck barely came to a stop before brushing the donkey's hide. Donkeys do not move out of the way on their own, but with the coaching of its master, this one finally moved into the brush, enabling us to get by.

The two men voiced questions about how to guide the people while encouraging them to lead themselves. "They say that we don't understand, because in a few years, we can just pack up and leave," Steve said to Matt. "But they are left with their relationships, and they don't want to scar them by telling other people what to do."

I was beginning to get sick from the roller coaster ride, but through the approaching nausea, I felt a small piece of the missionaries' heavy weight of responsibility and threatening discouragement. I remembered the empty church. I knew how tempting it would be for the missionary families to say, "Fine then, we'll leave and let you take care of your own problems. If we're not making an impact here, why bother giving up our American jobs and homes and families?"

After all, the mission had been in place for fifteen years, and there were still many problems in the community: weak leadership, feelings of entitlement, immorality, witchcraft, poor money management, basic ignorance about health, people refusing to care for their own family members.

As they talked and the Land Cruiser rocked down the path that no American county would call a road, I thought things over. I did not understand all the issues and questions of policy and disagreements. But I did understand that the missionaries in La Source were doing a good job of "leaving all personal belongings behind" in an attempt to save others.

Of course, most people forget from time to time that in the end we will all need to evacuate life. In the swirl of day-to-day schedules and coffee shop meetings and new machinery and baby showers and taking our vitamins, we think the "aircraft" we are on is too big and powerful to crash. Many people pay as much attention to their eternal destiny as air passengers give to the evacuation instructions on the screen. Other people do think about it and do what they can to honor God as they meet their schedules and take care of the details of daily life.

Here in La Source lived people who had grown up in the land of coffee shops and health food stores and world-class companies. The community of La Source knew this. The same people who begged for more and faced the consequences of their own choices and didn't want to be leaders—these people knew that the missionaries could have been back home living a life of comparative ease and comfort.

Instead, they saw Steve, throwing his laptop aside to make room for one more person.

The laptop being tossed aside to make room for one more

person symbolized many things. In its change of positions, I saw Nelson pouring a cement slab over the spring to keep the dirt from sliding down the mountain and contaminating the one source of pure water. I saw Rosemary stopping her laundry and cooking to feed a malnourished child whose brothers and sisters stole his food. I saw Matt and Sarah's family riding on donkeys when the truck got stuck, and Esther mourning her lost caterpillar. I saw Deborah going to a Haitian hospital to give birth. I saw Joanna washing the sores of a man dying of leprosy. I saw Bethanie sleeping on the cement hospital floor.

I caught my last glimpse of the orange Dr. Seuss flowers. Like the tiny community of missionaries in La Source, they were alone, just a speck on the vast landscape of Haiti. I began to wonder if the colorless background of white and brown and dusty green did not make the orange flowers even brighter. With a kind of Dr. Seuss humor, it was as if the orange flowers were laughing at the odds, laughing at the miserable setting, laughing at the poverty. *We are blessing more people here than the flowers in your nice flower beds,* they laughed, *because we are the only ones brave enough to be here.*

Every now and then Steve or Matt would look into the rearview mirror and call back a laughing string of Creole to the other passengers. The passengers would holler something back, and everyone smiled.

I knew that back at the hospital Bethanie and Joanna were making their rounds. Maybe Joanna was circling through the hospital with a Clorox bottle, making sure things were clean, or giving instructions to a new volunteer. Maybe Bethanie was working with an HIV patient or stopping to adjust a drip rate. Whatever they were doing, I knew they were smiling.

CHAPTER 25

SWITCHING WORLDS

While fields and floods, rocks, hills, and plains,
repeat the sounding joy . . .

I saw three children near Port-au-Prince, sitting on the flat
top of a stone wall. Just sitting, looking out over the landscape. Were they observing the roughness of the landscape,
or were they so used to it that they didn't notice its barren
beauty? Were they looking at the jet banking down toward
the airport, wondering if they would ever ride on one? Or
were they just sunning themselves on their little perch above
the tent cities, maybe making up stories like my brother and
I used to do?

On the outskirts of Port-au-Prince lies a massive soccer
field with huge lights and a couple of basketball courts tacked
on the side. In this field a group of earthquake victims had
recently played soccer against each other, my guides told
me. All the players were amputees; they played on crutches.
I wondered what the rules were. Could you hit the ball with
your crutch?

Getting close to Port-au-Prince, there are banana and
plantain fields and cows cropping grass beside the river.
In the city there are trees, loaded with wonderful lavender

flowers. My guides did not know what they were called. I decided it must be a geranium tree, because that was what the flowers looked like. In a pickup bed full of people, I saw a man playing a guitar. There was a campaign procession of motorcycles carrying people in white T-shirts with writing on the back that I could not read.

After a relatively short flight, we reached the Miami airport. As much as it lacks in organization, it is still a beautiful place. I noticed the gold sea creatures and shells embossed on the floors.

Then there was Chicago. I didn't remember it being so beautiful when I left. As the plane took a sharp curve above Lake Michigan and tilted in for the landing, the jeweled skyline reached up to greet us. Each skyscraper looked like a little toy that an organized child had put in place. It seemed likely that we could pluck one up as a souvenir, if only the pilot would bring us a little closer. Miles of Chicago streets stretched out in symmetrical city blocks, lighting the sky to the horizon.

In O'Hare's hall with the multi-story ceiling, extravagant wreaths and red bows still hung over the hurrying passengers, eight days after New Year. I saw a woman stop to take a picture.

Several days later I was back on my futon, eating Chili's leftovers from a Styrofoam takeout box, washing it down with a Pepsi One I had found in my refrigerator. I had a new niece, Alyssa, who had been born in Wisconsin that morning. I had nursing classes starting the next day. I had boys' and girls' club on Wednesday night.

Christmas vacation was over, and I was back in the whirlpool lifestyle of North America. However, I could not forget the healing, the simple atmosphere, the peace I had felt. I could not forget the blue hospital, nor the people who had spent their Christmas in it. *If they can take the time to serve God like that*, I said to myself, *I can take the time to tell their story.*

SOUP JOUMOU
(Haitian Pumpkin Soup)

Ingredients

1/2 lb. beef stew meat

1/2 lb. chicken

1 lb. pumpkin

1/2 lb. cabbage

3 medium potatoes

2 large carrots

1 onion

1/4 c. celery stalks and leaves

3 cloves

1 T. lime juice

1 whole goat pepper (or hot pepper)

1/4 lb. vermicelli pasta (or spaghetti)

4 c. water

Use a large kettle to boil the beef and chicken for 15–20 minutes with the lime juice and cloves. Remove any froth which forms. Add the vegetables and continue boiling until the meat becomes tender and the vegetables are cooked (about 45 more minutes). Turn off the heat and let cool. Cube the meat and puree the vegetables. Return the meat and puree to the kettle and bring to a boil, adding water if necessary. Add the vermicelli and the whole (uncut) hot pepper. Simmer until the vermicelli is tender.

PRONUNCIATION GUIDE

ankò	ahn KAW
bannann	BAH nahn
bonjou	BOH joo
bourik	BOO reek
Derilès	DEH ree lehs
dola	DOH lah
Dyelès	JYAY lehs
Gonaives	goh nah YEEV
Jidna	JEED nah
joumou	JOO moo
Kanès	kah NEHS
l'ap kite nou	lahp KEE tay nou
La Source	lah SOOS
m'ap mouri	MAHP MOO ree
mèsi	MEH see
Mizè	MEE zeh
pa souke	PAH SOO kay
pitimi	PEE tee mee
Sèntàn	SEHN tahn
Tata	TAH tah
Titanyen	TEE tah YEHN
Wadlè	WAHD leh
wi	WEE
Wozmika	wohz MEE kah

ABOUT THE AUTHOR

Katrina Hoover is a writer and nursing student from Goshen, Indiana. She grew up in Stratford, Wisconsin, with two brothers and three sisters, all of whom developed a love for words through the coaching and example of their parents. Katrina moved to Indiana in 2006, where she taught school before enrolling as a nursing student at Ivy Tech Community College. Her first book, *On the Winning Side,* was published in 2010 by Christian Light Publications. It focuses on the children's ministries she has been involved in, both in Wisconsin and Indiana. Although she has carried out many ideas in her life, writing *Blue Christmas* while in nursing school was the most adventurous one so far. She credits both the idea for the book and the strength to finish it to our all-knowing and creative God.

Katrina plans to graduate from nursing school in May 2011 and get a job where she can develop her newly-acquired skills. Other dreams of hers include raising black beef calves, traveling to England again, and donating a kidney, since no one has to have two of them.

Katrina enjoys hearing from readers and can be contacted at katrina@500-words.com. You may also write to her in care of Christian Aid Ministries, P.O. Box 360, Berlin, Ohio, 44610.

Christian Aid Ministries

Christian Aid Ministries was founded in 1981 as a nonprofit, tax-exempt 501(c)(3) organization. Its primary purpose is to provide a trustworthy and efficient channel for Amish, Mennonite, and other conservative Anabaptist groups and individuals to minister to physical and spiritual needs around the world. This is in response to the command ". . . do good unto all men, especially unto them who are of the household of faith" (Gal. 6:10).

Each year, CAM supporters provide approximately 15 million pounds of food, clothing, medicines, seeds, Bibles, Bible story books, and other Christian literature for needy people. Most of the aid goes to orphans and Christian families. Supporters' funds also help clean up and rebuild for natural disaster victims, put up Gospel billboards in the U.S., support several church-planting efforts, operate two medical clinics, and provide resources for needy families to make their own living. CAM's main purposes for providing aid are to help and encourage God's people and bring the Gospel to a lost and dying world.

CAM has staff, warehouse, and distribution networks in Romania, Moldova, Ukraine, Haiti, Nicaragua, Liberia, and Israel. Aside from management, supervisory personnel, and bookkeeping operations, volunteers do most of the work at CAM locations. Each year, volunteers at our warehouses, field bases, DRS projects, and other locations donate over 200,000 hours of work.

CAM's ultimate purpose is to glorify God and help enlarge His kingdom. ". . . whatsoever ye do, do all to the glory of God" (I Cor. 10:31).

Additional Books

God Knows My Size! / *by Harvey Yoder*
How God answered Silvia Tarniceriu's specific prayer
251 pages $10.99

They Would Not Be Silent / *by Harvey Yoder*
Testimonies of persecuted Christians in Eastern Europe
231 pages $10.99

They Would Not Be Moved / *by Harvey Yoder*
More testimonies of Christians who stood strong under communism
208 pages $10.99

Elena—Strengthened Through Trials / *by Harvey Yoder*
A young Romanian girl strengthened through hardships
240 pages $10.99

Where Little Ones Cry / *by Harvey Yoder*
The sad trails of abandoned children in Liberia during civil war
168 pages plus 16-page picture section $10.99

Wang Ping's Sacrifice / *by Harvey Yoder*
Vividly portrays the house church in China
191 pages $10.99

A Small Price to Pay / *by Harvey Yoder*
Mikhail Khorev's story of suffering under communism
247 pages $10.99

Tsunami!—*from a few that survived* / *by Harvey Yoder*
Survivors tell their stories, some with sorrow and heartbreak, others with joy and hope.
168 pages $11.99

Tears of the Rain / *by Ruth Ann Stelfox*
Poignantly honest account of a missionary family in war-torn Liberia
479 pages $13.99

A Greater Call / *by Harvey Yoder*
What will it cost Wei to spread the Gospel in China?
195 pages $11.99

Angels in the Night / *by Pablo Yoder*
The Pablo Yoder family's experiences in Waslala, Nicaragua
356 pages $12.99

The Happening / *by Harvey Yoder*
Nickel Mines school shooting—healing and forgiveness
173 pages $11.99

In Search of Home / *by Harvey Yoder*
The true story of a Muslim family's miraculous conversion
240 pages $11.99

HeartBridge / *by Johnny Miller*
Joys and sorrows at the Nathaniel Christian Orphanage
272 pages $12.99

A Heart to Belong / *by Johnny Miller*
A Heart to Belong (sequel to *HeartBridge*) continues the story of God's sustaining grace as the Millers love and guide the children of the Nathaniel Christian Orphanage in Romania.
302 pages $12.99

The Long Road Home / *by Pablo Yoder*
Will prayers and the Spirit's promptings bring young Pablo "home"?
456 pages $12.99

Miss Nancy / *by Harvey Yoder*
The fascinating story of God's work through the life of an Amish missionary in Belize
273 pages $11.99

Into Their Hands / *by Harvey Yoder*
Bible smugglers find ingenious ways to transport Bibles into Romania and the former Soviet Union.
194 pages $11.99

A Life Redeemed / *by Harvey Yoder*
The inspiring story of Ludlow Walker's journey from his childhood in Jamaica to his current calling as a minister of the Gospel. An unforgettable story of God's redeeming grace and transforming power.
232 pages $11.99

Bread for the Winter / *by Harvey Yoder*
Eight-year-old Pavel learns from his godly parents what Jesus meant when He said, "Love your enemies . . ."
72 pages $4.99

Jeremy's Garden / *by Valerie and Charity Miller*
Follow young Jeremy as he learns how to care for his garden. Excellent pencil drawings throughout the book make it appealing to young eyes.
40 pages $3.99

Vera, the King's Daughter / *by Harvey Yoder*
The story of this unlikely princess, set in the plains of central Ukraine, will inspire all who meet her through the pages of this book.
208 pages $11.99

Little Amazon / *by Lena Eicher*
When Franklin's parents decide to take a family trip to Belize, twelve-year-old Franklin isn't sure he wants to go. But the trip turns out to be filled with exciting and rewarding discoveries. Most important, Franklin learns about answered prayer and God's nearness far away from home.
80 pages $4.99

Out of the Depths / *by Rachael Lofgren*
Tragic events destroyed Ludmilla's security in her family structure and caused heart pain difficult to imagine. Broken and lonely, she arrives at a crossroad. Will she make the right decision? Readers will find themselves drawn into Ludmilla's story as she seeks answers.
240 pages $11.99

Shatterproof / *by Katrina Hoover*
Is anything in this world really *shatterproof?* You will be touched as you enter the lives of the characters who experienced catastrophes in the deadly tornado outbreaks of 2011 and faced the aftershock with courage and faith.
340 pages $12.99

The Way to God and Peace

We live in a world contaminated by sin. Sin is anything that goes against God's holy standards. When we do not follow the guidelines that God our Creator gave us, we are guilty of sin. Sin separates us from God, the source of life.

Since the time when the first man and woman, Adam and Eve, sinned in the Garden of Eden, sin has been universal. The Bible says that we all have "sinned and come short of the glory of God" (Romans 3:23). It also says that the natural consequence for that sin is eternal death, or punishment in an eternal hell: "Then when lust hath conceived, it bringeth forth sin: and sin, when it is finished, bringeth forth death" (James 1:15).

But we do not have to suffer eternal death in hell. God provided forgiveness for our sins through the death of His only Son, Jesus Christ. Because Jesus was perfect and without sin, He could die in our place. "For God so loved the world that he gave his only begotten Son, that whosoever believeth in him should not perish, but have everlasting life" (John 3:16).

A sacrifice is something given to benefit someone else. It costs the giver greatly. Jesus was God's sacrifice. Jesus' death takes away the penalty of sin for everyone who accepts this sacrifice and truly repents of their sins. To repent of sins means to be truly sorry for and turn away from the things we have done that have violated God's standards. (Acts 2:38; 3:19).

Jesus died, but He did not remain dead. After three days, God's Spirit miraculously raised Him to life again. God's Spirit does something similar in us. When we receive Jesus as our sacrifice and repent of our sins, our hearts are changed. We become spiritually alive! We develop new desires and attitudes (2 Corinthians 5:17). We begin to make choices that please God (1 John 3:9). If we do fail and commit sins, we can ask God for forgiveness. "If we confess our sins, he is faithful and just to forgive us our sins, and to cleanse us from all unrighteousness" (1 John 1:9).

Once our hearts have been changed, we want to continue growing spiritually. We will be happy to let Jesus be the Master of our lives and will want to become more like Him. To do this, we must meditate on God's Word and commune with God in prayer. We will testify to others of this change by being baptized and sharing the good news of God's victory over sin and death. Fellowship with a faithful group of believers will strengthen our walk with God (1 John 1:7).